DATE DUE

MAR 2 5 1985			
AUG 9 1985			
FEB. 7 1987			

Family / Parenting

THE UNWANTED GENERATION

Meier, Paul D.
Burnett, Linda

DEMCO

The
Unwanted
Generation

The Unwanted Generation

A Guide to Responsible Parenting

Paul D. Meier
and
Linda Burnett

BAKER BOOK HOUSE
Grand Rapids, Michigan

To *my Mother*
Irene Laptad Holmes
and my Father
Eugene Julius Holmes
Only in heaven will they realize
the full extent of my
love and appreciation for them (1 Cor. 13:12).

Linda Burnett

Contents

Acknowledgments

I am grateful to my loving husband, Bill, who supported and encouraged me through my research and writing, not only generally, but specifically by his willingness to watch the children while I worked on this book.

I am grateful as well to others in my circle of family and friends who lovingly cared for my sons and enabled me to find additional time for research and writing—my parents, Eugene and Irene Holmes, my parents-in-law, Frances and Clell Burnett, and my friends Mary Jane Crossland and Elizabeth Mayhew.

For contributing thoughts and ideas and assisting in finding material for the book, I am indebted to Judy Freeman, Dr. Mike Griffey, Mary Ann Miller, and Ethel Roberts. I am thankful, too, for the prayer support of Irene and Rick Proctor, Lisa Powell, and Joy White.

And, I express my thanks to Anita Brice and Denise Kerbo who helped in typing the manuscript and to Moka Lambert, Cherly Morris Wood, and Debbie Lloyd, who assisted in other final stages of the script.

Linda Burnett

Introduction

Today I am rejoicing because eight-year-old Mary has been snatched from the unwanted generation and returned to her rightful place as a wanted child. Both her self-worth and behavior are improving already, and the entire course of Mary's life will be altered.

Rescuing Mary from the unwanted generation was not easy. It took many gracious interventions—by a loving God, an elementary school teacher, a pastor, three psychiatrists (including myself), two parents willing to repent of their selfishness, and an insecure eight-year-old willing to demonstrate faith in herself and God. What happened to Mary is typical of many cases that prompted Linda Burnett (a Christian housewife and conference speaker) and myself (a Christian psychiatrist) to write this book.

Mary had behavior problems although her parents are attractive, middle-aged, upper-middle class, hard-working people who attended a solid evangelical church regularly. Mary's elementary school teacher noticed repeatedly that something about Mary was different—she seemed insecure. At various times she was brash, irritable, hyperactive, and very sad. Mary's teacher finally recommended that Mary's parents be advised to seek psychiatric help for their daughter.

Mary's parents, who suspected as much subconsciously, were nevertheless embarrassed to face the prospect that their daughter could possibly have serious psychological problems. Their pride was hurt. They followed the advice of school officials, however, and brought Mary to my office. For an hour I chatted alone with Mary and asked her to answer a number of vital questions. A brief neurological exam assured me that her behavior problems were not organic (caused by physical problems). After that, I began my usual process—psychotherapy on Mary's parents until Mary got better. A child's problems (unless the child has some physical problem) usually reflect the parents' personal hangups and inferior child-rearing techniques.

After I insisted, Mary's mother and father agreed to undergo thorough psychological testing and begin work on their own hangups, while Mary was receiving help for hers. When I first explained the procedure, they were disappointed. They wanted me to "cure" their daughter and not delve into their own personal lives. They resented the implication that the responsibility for causing *and* curing Mary's hangups laid squarely on their own shoulders.

At first, each parent denied having serious, personal problems. Finally, the husband admitted that they did have a few marital conflicts. Psychological testing, however, revealed that both parents were filled with false pride, self-centeredness, self-righteous attitudes, and a fear of intimacy. The testing further revealed that Mary's mother was acutely depressed and anxious.

Further probing by two other psychiatrists and me revealed that Mary's mother had not really wanted this pregnancy. From the first, Mary was an unwanted child. From infancy, Mary was placed in a day-care center nine hours a day, five days a week. They used "meeting little Mary's material needs" as self-righteous justification for leaving her in the day-care center.

They had no idea how much psychological damage a child can experience from excessive time spent in a day-care center. They had no idea that they had placed their daughter in the unwanted generation.

As intensive therapy continued, Mary's mother confessed an extramarital affair over many years with a man at her job. She initially felt guilty about her affair (she was a Christian), but had become increasingly hardened to her sin as she persisted in it. In therapy, she denied feeling much guilt; but psychological testing revealed considerable repressed guilt. She was deceiving herself.

Through encouragement from three Christian psychiatrists and her pastor, she became aware of the extensive guilt she was repressing. She gave up the affair. She decided to choose to love her husband, and after a week or two of behaving in love toward him, her love for him returned for the first time in ten years. Her husband repented of his sins also, and began spending less time working and more time communicating with his wife and child.

For the first time in Mary's life, her parents accepted her as a *wanted child*. Mary will carry a few permanent psychological scars after spending eight years in the unwanted generation of children, but most of her hangups were resolved through the repentance and hard work of her parents. Thank God, her parents were willing to face up to their sins and false piety and commit their lives to God, to each other, and to Mary.

A case such as Mary's would have been unusual for a psychiatrist a generation or two ago. But we are living in a different age—an age when the feminist movement is being carried to an extreme. Although one should fight to diminish male chauvinism and unfairness to women in our culture, we must remain on guard against the sinful extremes of some liberationists in their intense reaction to the chauvinism of the past. Too frequently being a housewife is labeled a form of slavery. Too many women are hearing the message that wives are inferior and that only fulltime career women are real successes. A child is viewed as an obstacle, a handicap, a bore, a chore, a curse, or an accident. Children are becoming society's responsibility rather than the parent's concern. Too many children are being farmed out, like Mary was, to day-care centers, although research studies have shown how psychologically damaging forty or fifty hours a week in a day-care center can be to children during those crucial first six years of their lives. Children today are living in an unwanted generation, and we will suffer the consequences both as individual parents and as a nation.

In 1976, Ann Landers polled her millions of readers with the question, "If you had it to do over again, would you have children?" Mrs. Landers, herself a mother and grandmother, was surprised that 70 percent of those who responded said no. By writing *The Unwanted Generation*, Linda Burnett and I express our hope that couples planning marriage *will not have* children unless they really want them, or, if they do want them, that they decide to rear their children responsibly. We challenge parents with children at home to the God-given responsibility of providing personal and loving care for them.

Paul Meier, M.D.

1

A Housewife's Perspective

I felt sick as I got off the phone. Janet had just asked me if I knew of a job opening somewhere. She has two children the same age as my two (both under three). One of her statements kept going through my mind: "We couldn't have this particular house if I didn't work; we think it's worth it." Then she began to praise the day-care center where she had already started leaving her girls.

The pattern is familiar. It seems that the minute a young mother tells me she's working she begins to praise the particular day-care center her children attend—why it's better than the others. I'm sure that many of these women have convinced themselves that their children are actually better off there than at home with them.

I have many friends and acquaintances whose children are left for others to raise. I have a tremendous burden of concern for these parents as well as for their children.

As mothers we will have our children at home under our primary care for only four or five years. Eighty-five percent of their personalities will be formed by the time they are six! What do I know about the day-care personnel who would shape the attitudes and self-worth of my children if left in their care? It is nearly impossible for a day-care worker to treat my children with the same love and patience that I would. She doesn't *love* my children like I do—even if she *does* love children in general (which isn't always the case). Consequently, I am certain that my children would not develop the confidence and security, on which they will depend throughout their lives, to the same extent at a day-care center that they would at home. There seldom is an adequate substitute for the real parent.

Visiting with an out-of-town friend recently left me depressed. She had just finished telling me all about her exciting new career when I asked her whether her three-year-old son was too much trouble to take care of in between all her hours at work and the little time left to do house work and cooking. "My no!" was her reply, "At this day-care center they taught him how to eat and walk, and they even potty trained him!"

I can't imagine not being in on some of the most important moments of my children's infant stages. For my friend, was there someone there at the day-care center to really reinforce her baby's attitudes for future achievements? Was someone there to make him feel like he had really accomplished something—to make him feel *special?* Each child in this world needs encouragement to feel special—to being something more than just part of a group. What our children learn in the first few years (especially before age four), they will carry and depend on throughout adulthood.

Remember Janet's phone call? Well, I didn't say anything to her at the time. But when I got off the phone, after thinking a while, I went into the bedroom to talk to Bill, my husband. I asked him: "Am I all washed up?" Is it "different strokes for different folks"—even concerning our children? Is what's good for one child not good for another? Then, after some discussion and no firm conclusions, I felt driven to search for the answer myself—both in God's word and by discovering what psychologists and sociologists say.

Two days later Janet called back. After telling me about her summer job, she continued, "The bad thing about it is that I won't get to see my children for three months. I'll be working from seven in the morning to ten at night." At that point I could no longer resist telling her how I really felt. "You won't see much more of them the rest of the year if you get another job." Then I began enumerating the reasons why a mother should stay at home. "But," she said, "there are so many unsaved people in the world . . . a Christian witness is needed where I work." My answer to her was the same one the woman with six children received after she told her country preacher that she had been "called to preach." "Wonderful!" the preacher responded, "now go on home to your congregation."

Raising a child in our day is both the most difficult and rewarding task God calls a woman to do. I recently read a newspaper editorial that said, "Women who stay at home show a callous, self-interest." I would have laughed if I hadn't been so physically and emotionally drained after caring for my two boys all day, along with cooking and cleaning. I must admit that I've been tempted to follow the crowd by placing my children in a day-care center and going to a job where I could interact with *adults* all day long. As I called my husband one day at work, I overheard him, his associate, and secretary laughing about something as he answered the phone. My heart tugged as I immediately reacted, "Boy, would I love to get in on that!" But when Bill calls me, it's a different story. It's not unusual for him to interrupt my changing a diaper while my other child is clamoring for my attention.

But, it's worth it! Every minute of it. I have the satisfaction of knowing that I'm doing what the Lord wants me to do, and I'm reaping the fruits of obedience already: the unexpected flower brought in from outdoors, the spontaneous kisses, and the joy of hearing Brian answer, "Jesus," when I ask him who made the flowers.

One of my friends was married when she was seventeen. Brenda's first baby came a year later, and by the time she was twenty-three she had four children. "How did you do it?" I asked her. "I cried nearly every day," she said. It astounds me that anyone could consider someone like Brenda "callous and selfish." I kept praising her for what she had accomplished by raising four children at home. She told me later that soon after talking to me, she told her husband, "You married some powerful woman!" I agree.

As a Christian woman with the power of Jesus Christ living in me (the same power that God used to raise Him from the dead, according to Eph. 1:20) I can have not only real victory in the area of child rearing, but joy as well.

The infant stages of our children's lives are brief and yet the most important both psychologically and sociologically. After they are little, we will never again have a comparable opportunity to shape the lives of our children for good.

Brenda now has four happy, well-adjusted teenagers. "I don't think my kids would be worth anything if I hadn't raised them. Not, because of me," she continued, "but because of the security they found in the unity of our home."

Dr. Howard Hendricks, a prominent Christian author, cites a questionnaire in which a group of young couples were asked to list their priorities. Most of the lists started with "a nice house" and other material possessions, with relationships listed toward the bottom. Twenty years later the same people were asked to rewrite their priorities, and almost all of them put relationships first—especially with their children. Some of these parents are now trying to pick up the broken pieces of their lives—the consequences of their previous shallow priorities.

I mourn for the women of my generation who will look back too late, and think, "Oh, if only I could live this part of my life over again." I hope that many mothers will change the direction of their family life and avoid unnecessary heartbreaks in the years to come.

Linda Burnett

Psychiatric Comment

Currently, over 60 percent of American mothers are on the American labor force. Many, but not all of them, have bought the "day-care center philosophy" of child-rearing. The children of these mothers, whether the parents admit it or not, are part of "the unwanted generation." They are the generation of children who "get in the way" and are considered as obstacles by their career-oriented mothers and materialistic fathers. They will suffer the results of low self-concepts, and many will rebel. Proverbs 29:15 says, ". . . a child left to itself disgraces his mother."

As a psychiatrist, I have seen the story in the following illustration occur over and over again, but usually not with as good results:

Of all life's pressures, none is harder to bear than trouble at home. Financial pressure is tough but not impossible to work out. Physical pain is bad—sometimes horrible—but usually not without hope. The loss of a job or failure at school may bring to the surface those feelings of desperation, yet they, too, will pass. But there is really nothing to compare with the lingering, agonizing, torturous heartache brought on by a rebellious and wayward child. Too big to spank. Too angry to reason with. Too volatile to threaten. Too stubborn to warn. Bound and determined to run free of authority . . . regardless. The rebel has one great desire in life (to borrow from Sinatra's gold platter)—to say:

". . . I did it *my* way."

Maddened with an adventurous lust for excitement, anxious to burst from the tight cocoon of parental control, the young anarchist creates havoc in a home before finally deciding to fly wild and free. Soon it occurs. With the slam of a door. "I'm gone forever!"

At that moment, a bittersweet relief is felt by both sides. But not for long. At home, a measure of peace returns, but soon silence mates with memories, bearing the crippled offspring of guilt, grief, and shame.

A foolish son is a grief to his father and bitterness to her who bore him. (Prov. 17:25)

If you have been there, no one needs to elucidate. The brokenhearted mom and dad need a comforter not a commentator. It is agony at its highest peak. Imagination, like the rebel, runs wild, as worry and fear and empathy play mental music in a minor key.

Time drags. No word. The chill of winter and the rains of spring merely widen the chasm of silence. No word. Summer's furnace and fall's colors do little to temper the edge of parental anxiety. No word. Prayer becomes a lonely vigil... at times, an empty, hopeless, repetition of sounds struggling out of a swollen face. Thoughts are confused and endless.

Where did we go wrong... ?
Will we ever see each other again... ?
Is he/she safe... ?
If we had it to do over again...
How did it all start... ?
Should we... could we... ?

Still no word.
Winter returns... but not the wayward. Its icy blast pushes its way through windows and doors... but the phone doesn't ring and a knock doesn't come. No familiar voice breaks the silence.

Suddenly. Unannounced. At the least expected moment, the prodigal comes back... back to where life makes up its mind. Home.

A lean profile can be seen on the horizon. Shoulders are stooped. Head bowed. Long lines of remorse, disgrace, humiliation stretch across that once-defiant face. Wasted and repentant, with only a few soft-spoken whispers of apology... the wayward lad slumps into the arms of the waiting dad. As time momentarily stops. And two hearts beat together again. One forgiving, the other forgiven.[1]

After counseling hundreds of families like the one in this illustration, I urge parents to adopt good child-rearing habits now, rather than hoping for a major turnaround by their children later. According to most research findings as well as my own personal experiences, *most* human beings will not change more than 15 percent after their sixth birthday. Thank God, miracles do occur, but don't count on a miracle in your child's life.

Paul Meier, M.D.

Notes

1. Chuck Swindoll, *News-Break* (weekly publication of the First Evangelical Free Church, Fullerton, Calif.).

2

If It Feels Good, Do It!

"If it feels good, do it!" This prevailing philosophy of life that characterizes our generation is the same philosophy of the Epicureans in Christ's day—that personal happiness is the highest good. "Do your own thing" is the modern way of life for many Americans.

Too many children in our day are not taught self*less*ness or responsibility. Perhaps the problem is that they are not taught much at all at home by their parents. They are left at day-care centers whose main job is to keep bottoms dry and tummies full. Even our schools cannot adequately replace the home for building character. The primary place where children *can* learn character is in the home. Just as children cannot grow spiritually just by attending Sunday School one hour a week, neither will they learn duty, reliability, kindness, and sacrifice by spending only a short amount of time with mommy and daddy at the breakfast and dinner table.

Many parents simply have not outgrown the infant stage themselves. The transition from childlessness to parenthood is difficult and major. Many young couples lack the maturity required. Michael Novak, stated it aptly when he said, "Children are not a welcome responsibility, for to have children is plainly to cease being a child oneself."[1]

While at the park with my two boys one afternoon, I

noticed some other mothers with their little ones. One little girl stood out because of her big blue eyes and blond hair (I always thought "my" little girl would look like that). Becoming acquainted with her mother, I found that she worked from 8:00 a.m. to 5:00 p.m. five days a week. "Boy, I'll bet you really miss her!" I said. "Oh, no," she replied. Noticing how surprised I looked, she explained, "You see, I went right back to work three weeks after she was born, so I never really got used to being with her long enough to miss her now."

Apparently, some people decide to have a baby for the same reasons that others buy a dog. They think that a baby is merely someone to play with. They do not anticipate the awesome and totally consuming responsibility a child creates. Perhaps these couples should buy a dog instead—it would require less care, and, if neglected, the magnitude of the consequences would be far less.

This parental unpreparedness is not entirely the fault of parents. We are bombarded daily with this epicurean philosophy. On a Mother's Day, in a hometown paper, I noticed an obvious example. The leading article in the women's section praised the role of motherhood, but right under it was another article under the heading, "WORK WANTED! AMBITIOUS WOMEN SEEKING SATISFACTORY JOBS, SURVIVAL." In the article, an "employability instructor" said, "people want a job not necessarily for the money but for the personal fulfillment." Further on in the article she encouraged women, "At some time when you take charge of your life you're going to say, It means more to me what I think about myself than what anyone else thinks about me. *You have to be extremely selfish*" [italics mine].

In a TV advertisement a woman says, "Frankly, I'm worth it!" And another commercial doesn't even try to be subtle wherein a woman states emphatically, "I'm doing this for *number one!*" Television may not be the only bad influence but it is unquestionably the most influential. Many social analysts are convinced that TV has moved ahead of home, church, and school as the principle influence on morality. Researchers have found that by the time an American child reaches eighteen, he has spent twenty-thousand hours before the TV set—more than he does in the classroom.[2]

Much of this self-gratification syndrome is manifested in the big push to encourage the housewife and mother to get out of the home. This is propagandized as fulfillment. At first the main thrust was largely by militant feminists, but it has subtly seeped into the subconsciousness of the average homemaker.

How often have you heard a woman, when asked what she does, reply, "Oh, I'm just a housewife." I do not believe that the "just" feeling was put upon her by male chauvinists only, but as well by women out on the working force who feel that most other women should join them. Because some women could not find fulfillment and a sense of purpose in the roles of a homemaker, wife, and mother, they have taken it upon themselves to make sure no other woman does. They portray the homemaker as selfish, callous, and lazy for not working or as one to be pitied because she is trapped in her own house.

A friend of mine who attended our state's International Womens' Year Conference said that among much of the biased material presented was a particular film depicting the men as villains and the woman as victims. After viewing the movie, she was ready to go home and pick a fight with her husband. This "inspiration" she got was no mistake. That was the purpose of the film and of most of the material. Betty Friedan alludes to the homemaker's role in these terms:

> But is her house in reality a comfortable concentration camp? Have not women who live in the image of the feminine mystique trapped themselves within the narrow walls of their homes? They have learned to "adjust" to their sociological role. They have become dependent, passive, childlike; they have given up their adult frame of reference to live at the lower level of food and things. The work they do does not require adult capabilities, it is endless, monotonous, unrewarding.[3]

When a mother of a newborn daughter decided to quit her job, she confided to Carolyn Lewis, "The women in the office are furious with me. They think I'm selling out." Hurt by the antagonism of her female colleagues, she was troubled by her decision. This was Carolyn's reaction:

> Our conversation brought to the surface the growing uneasiness I have been feeling about the Women's Movement. In our eagerness to exact equal treatment, we women seem to be forgetting who we are. We are not men. Men cannot bear children . . . Here is a tiny, talcumed ball of potential, the whole luminous future of the universe, waiting to be loved and shaped. There is nothing either inconsequential or demeaning about choosing to make this child one's life work. Nor is there anything shameful in wanting to make life comfortable and happy for another human, like a husband.[4]

My Personal Emancipation Proclamation

One evening I heard a speech on marriage that strengthened my views on family life. But it especially affected how I viewed my eighteen-month-old son. This woman emphasized that some go into marriage expecting to retain the same freedoms and engage in the same activities they enjoyed when they were single. But they shouldn't—they're *not* single. They have made a commitment to a marriage partner, and part of that commitment involves sacrificing some of the former lifestyle.

Similarly, many parents after having children maintain the idea that their lifestyle shouldn't differ from what it was before they had children. But it *should*. They now have a responsibility and moral obligation to another human being.

Hearing that speaker, listening to my mother-in-law, and conversing with my sister-in-law revolutionized the way I had been living. My sister-in-law wasn't actually talking about her kids when she told me about a party she attended. She had taken her boys, and she said to me, "When we arrived, I got them started in playing a game, and when I knew they were happy, then I could go and enjoy the party myself." As she shared this with me it really shook me (although, I didn't show it). It was so contrary to the way I had been thinking. If I had to take my son to a party, I would have thought: "Brian had better behave and not keep me from having a good time."

Of course, I love my son. I just would not want him to interfere with *my* plans, *my* activities, and *my* lifestyle.

At times, the Lord tells me something not only once, but He takes me through a period of time confronting me repeatedly with the same truth, even though it comes through different people saying different things. But these insights lead me to one conclusion.

When Brian, my firstborn, was eighteen months old I became aware that I viewed him as an inconvenience—an intruder into my lifestyle. At that point I made a commitment to put his happiness and welfare above mine, and I asked Jesus to continually remind me of it. I cannot express the *freedom* that came with that commitment. Instead of considering Brian as a barrier to daily goals—he *was* my main goal. If I spent my day meeting his needs, regardless whether my personal goals came fourth or fifth on my "things to do list," I had accomplished something important. I felt fulfilled in knowing that I gave him the love and security he'll need now as well as when he becomes an adult. Amazingly, some of his demands and activities that formerly irritated me (because they interfered with what *I* was doing) didn't seem to bother me as they had done before. I began to enjoy just being around him. I praise God that my emancipation came before my second son, John Mark, was born when Brian was twenty months old.

I am saddened to think of how many young mothers are now in the frame of mind I was in during my year-and-a-half of viewing Brian as an "intruder." I hurt even more for the children who will bear emotional scars into adulthood because of it. Bill and I have given these potential scars in Brian's life to God, trusting Him to heal and to use us now in giving Brian all the love and security that he'll need for the future. We claimed God's promise: "Then I will repay you for the years that the locust has eaten..." (Joel 2:25).

Ironically, people who do, take, and buy for themselves are doing it in seeking happiness, when true happiness is found only in doing for and giving to others. The biblical principle is clear: "Give and it shall be given to you. A good measure, pressed down, shaken together, and running over, will be poured into your lap. For with the measure you use, it will be measured to you" (Luke 6:38).

Self-gratification isn't the only erroneous idea prevalent in our society. Another myth seeping into our ideology is that we, as individuals, are not responsible for our foibles and shortcomings.

A counselor at a small Christian college in Arkansas shared this experience about one of his students. Single, she was pregnant for the second time by the same boy (she aborted the first baby). But she was angry at *society*. Because of the high cost of living, she asserted that she would be unable to keep the baby. She felt it was society's fault for the situation she created in the first place. The father of this baby assumed no responsibility whatsoever.

Children easily pass the blame for something they do wrong. And some grownups, as well, never reach a time in their lives when they own up to their mistakes. "The Devil made me do it," quipped Flip Wilson in jest. But some Christians say it in all seriousness.

As adults we should realize that although our environments were factors in forming our basic personalities, and although we may have been placed in tough situations, we must assume responsibility for our choices and "own up" to them if they were the wrong ones.

It's exciting to know that we as Christians don't *have* to make the wrong decisions anymore. For the first time in our lives we have the power to make the right choices now that we are "new creations" (2 Cor. 5:17). God Himself, in the person of the Holy Spirit, is willing to do anything through us that's according to His will. He never calls us

to do anything that He is not willing to do *in* us.
"... Christ in you the hope of glory" (Col. 1:27).

But God's work in our lives is limited if we don't "own up" to our mistakes. We must *confess* our sins before God and repent, which means "to turn" or change direction (cf. 1 John 1:9). Then we can confidently move out in His power. We, as Paul, can say, "I can do everything through [Christ] who gives me strength (Phil. 4:13)."

The opposite of irresponsibility is claiming self-sufficiency, which is also repugnant to God. To say we do not need God is to set ourselves up as our own God. The phrase, "God helps those who help themselves," is not found in the Bible, although it has been quoted as "gospel." Actually Benjamin Franklin said it. But the message in Scripture is contrary to his famous quote. Basically, the biblical theme over and over is that God helps the helpless. "God opposes the proud, but gives grace to the humble" (James 4:6). Elsewhere, Paul says of God, "But He said to me, 'My grace is sufficient for you, for my power is made perfect in weakness'" (2 Cor. 12:9).

When Paul said "I can do everything through [Christ] ..." (Phil. 4:13), he was not asserting that he could do all things *for* Christ. There is no way that we can, in our own strength, live the Christian life. If Christ had come to this earth just to be an example, Christians would have to be pitied above all people. But He didn't. He came to die that we might live now and forever—"and the life I live in the body, I live by faith in the Son of God... (Gal. 2:20)."

Linda Burnett

Psychiatric Comment

When a woman goes out to work fulltime, leaving preschool children at a day-care center, she is likely to have genuine feelings of guilt. Like most humans, she is likely to repress her guilt feelings, rationalizing that they are based on old-fashioned morals. Also, she *might* socialize with women who encourage her to keep working. This could facilitate the repression of her guilt even further. When she meets a friend who happens to be a dedicated, fulltime mother, however, her repressed guilt may threaten to surface. To keep it repressed, she may feel compelled to persuade this dedicated mother into getting a job. After all, if she can talk a dedicated mother into going to work and leaving her children at a day-care center, then it must be morally justifiable.

In contrast, another mother with children under age six may falsely feel guilty for leaving her children at a nursery school or "mother's day out" program just several half-days per week. In reality, such breaks would likely make a better mother out of her. But since her false guilt prohibits her from doing what is best, and since "misery loves company," she is likely to feel self-righteously angry (she'll call it "frustrated" or "disappointed" rather than angry, however) toward women who don't have children or toward housewives who leave their children several hours at a time to pursue other creative activities.

The issue should not be "What will my parents think," "What will my church-friends think," or "What will the girls at the office think." The issue should be, "What alternative lifestyle will be most beneficial for my children. What would God want me to do for my husband, my children, and myself?"

Staying home twenty-four hours a day, day after day, doing household chores and taking care of several young children would be, in my opinion, too demanding for most people. After staying home occasionally with my four children all day to give my wife a day off, I know how demanding and frustrating child care can be. Doing a good job of parenting all day is stressful and difficult for most people, including myself, and I love my children dearly. Although I love them with all my heart, there are times when I get so angry at them that I have an urge to punch them even though I have never done so and never plan to. I don't know of many normal, married couples, Christian or non-Christian, who don't feel the same way at times. Exceptions to this are grandparents, who have by now forgotten what parenting felt like and have convinced themselves that they and their children have been nearly perfect.

I have, as a Christian psychiatrist, assured you that the frustrations of being a housewife are normal and that feeling angry at your children at times is also normal. But does this justify leaving your children in a day-care center and getting a full-time job? Absolutely not. That would be illogical, especially after considering the permanent, emotional damage that full-time day-care can cause to children. It would be more harmful to do that than it would be for mothers and children to stay cooped up in the house twenty-four hours a day, seven days a week. Both options are, in my opinion, detrimental to both your own and your children's mental health.

What is best for your children is also best for you. A mature person learns to delay self-gratification when necessary. As you grow older, it will be very important for you to be able to look back on your life and feel that you have done a good job of rearing your own children, although no parents are perfect.

But if you follow the Epicurean philosophy and impulsively make decisions based on selfish desires or frustrations, you will eventually harvest the adverse consequences.

Paul Meier, M.D.

Notes

1. Michael Novak, "The Family Is the Future," *Reader's Digest*, March 1978, p. 112.

2. *U.S. News & World Report*, 13 October 1975, p. 40.

3. Betty Friedan, *The Feminine Mystique* (New York: W. W. Norton & Co., 1968), p. 298.

4. Carolyn Lewis, "A Different Sort of Liberation," *Reader's Digest*, March 1978, p. 118.

3

The Importance of Infancy

Theodore Lidz, Chairman of the Department of Psychiatry at Yale University School of Medicine, states emphatically that "during no other period of life is the person so transformed both physically and developmentally as during infancy."[1] He further affirms that "no part of his life experience will be as solidly incorporated in the individual, become so irrevocably a part of him, as his infancy."[2] Lack of physical care can result in ill health, wasting away, and death. Lack of social nurturing will result in distortions of emotional development and stunting of intellectual growth.

Even an improper diet can influence the infant's lifetime intellectual capacity, since all of the nerve and brain cells a person will ever have are produced by six months of age.[3] After six months of age, brain cells may continue to enlarge, but no additional cells will ever be formed. That's why infants need plenty of protein, which they get primarily from milk during those first six months of life. Some mothers in ghetto areas have substituted liquids such as Kool-Aid for milk in their babies' bottles (since they could not afford much milk), which produced fewer brain cells in their children, limiting their mental capacities for the rest of their lives. Consequently, programs like Head Start are usually too late. During those first six months the infant's physical needs predominate. During the remainder of infancy, socialization and affection become important as well.

The human infant is among the most helpless and dependent of all of God's creatures. Too little support can leave the infant struggling for emotional survival, whereas too much support can lead the infant to become overly dependent. Gary Collins, a Christian psychologist, summarizes development during infancy as "characterized by rapid physical growth, initial perceptual and intellectual development, a learning to cope with new experiences, early social and emotional development, and the beginnings of personality formation."[4]

The Importance of
Stimulation and Experience in Infancy

The Four Basic Drives

Human beings have four basic drives: (1) tissue drives, such as the need for oxygen, water, and food; (2) sexual drives; (3) defensive drives—primarily fear and aggression, which Walter B. Cannon labeled the "fight or flight" mechanism; and (4) drives for stimulation and activity.

Spitz's Study on Marasmus

During World War II, a number of infants were placed in a European foundling home. Their mothers were allowed to stay with them during the first three months of life. During this time the infants developed normally. Then, apart from their mothers, they were cared for by nurses at a ratio of one nurse for eight to twelve infants. Good food was available, and the infants received good medical attention. But the nurses were busy, and the infants experienced very little stimulation through being held or handled. From this lack of stimulation, many stopped eating. About 30 percent of the babies died of malnutrition within the first year. Most of the survivors were not only unable to stand, walk, or talk by the age of four, but also had become mentally retarded.[5] This condition, in which an infant refuses to eat and becomes more and more emaciated, is known as *marasmus* (pronounced ma-raz'-mus). It is the failure to thrive, and occurs frequently, even in the United States. Research shows that many parents of infants suffering from marasmus are physically abusive, with a high incidence of alcoholic fathers. Many of these infants must be legally removed from their homes to be reared in foster homes. If caught in time and if given a lot of physical stimulation, some of these infants may partially recover and live relatively normal lives thereafter.[6]

Duke's "TV Kid"

A small, emaciated six-year-old boy, whose mother worked long hours, was left every day with his maternal grandmother. Unfortunately, the grandmother couldn't tolerate children, so she placed him in a crib every day from infancy, alone in a small room in front of a TV set. The child's only company was the TV set, except when his grandmother came in and set food in his crib. By the age of six, the emaciated boy was the size of an average three-year-old. He could not communicate, except for parroting TV commercials, which he did repeatedly. When a child psychiatrist at Duke Hospital asked him questions, he would spout off another TV commercial accurately. Various people worked with the boy extensively, but he was permanently handicapped both physically and mentally. The mother was rehabilitated, and the child was eventually returned to her custody. He was nicknamed "The TV Kid." Unfortunately, child neglect is not a rarity in America today. I know of numerous unmarried mothers on welfare who have as many as sixteen or eighteen children. They draw large welfare checks while their children roam the streets.

Animal Studies

The importance of the right kinds of stimulation has also been demonstrated in various animals. Dogs, for instance, restricted as pups by being raised in cages, developed striking abnormalities of behavior by the time they reached maturity.[7] When these same dogs were allowed to leave their cages after reaching full growth, they exhibited excessive behavioral arousal—they became overly excited by anything new in their environment. They broke into whirling fits so violent that they frequently bumped the walls, scraping the skin off their heads. They also exhibited impairment of selective perceptual processes—they ran around the room from one object to another, rarely showing sustained attention to a single object. They also had considerable difficulty getting along with normally reared dogs placed in their area. Another interesting study showed that rats handled daily and early in life developed much more vigorous antibody response to infections than did rats deprived of physical handling early in life.[8] In the animal kingdom, as well as in human existence, the adult's emotional condition and personality are strongly influenced by the amount and quality of stimulation received during infancy.[9]

Mother Substitutes

Mothers in the American Labor Force

Nearly 60 percent of American mothers are in the labor force, either part-time or full-time. The problem of "mother substitutes" is increasingly crucial. One study showed that

> the loss of mother is disturbing to an infant and produces a searching, agitated response. Substitute mothering can re-

lieve the distress, the extent depending in part on the degree of mothering provided and in part on the specific nature of the tie to mother.[10]

Further, if the loss of the infant's mother is not relieved

the infant soon lapses into a state of severe depression and withdrawal that appears to conserve his resources and minimize the danger of injury.[11]

Piaget's Findings

Jean Piaget's studies indicate that although adequate mother substitutes are satisfactory the first six months of life or so, on the social level the mother is very specifically needed by the infant starting about seven months of age.[12] Infants then need their own mothers for security and socialization, or a variable extent of permanent emotional and intellectual damage will occur. To summarize, before the child is seven or eight months of age, another competent person can be substituted for the mother without serious consequences, but not very readily after that age.

Unconditional Acceptance

Dr. Eugene McDanald states that "the mother's unconditional acceptance of the infant is the precursor to healthy self-acceptance which enables him to make the most of himself within the framework of his personal strengths and limitations, both physical and mental."[13] He further adds that "the child who has been unconditionally loved has a good conscience, experiences normal anxiety, and is relatively free in his choice of action."[14] On the other hand, the infant who has been conditionally loved has as he grows older, "a restrictive or a 'bad' conscience and experiences undue quantities of anxiety, hostility, and guilt which engenders various forms of compulsive behavior of a social or antisocial character."[15] By the time a child is old enough to go to school, most of his character structure has been established. An emotionally healthy, reflective child will be greatly enriched by this new contact with peers, teacher, and information. The anxiety-laden child, however, who fears the unknown will feel threatened by new interpersonal and environmental relationships. McDanald has wisely remarked, "The person who reaches adulthood with the feeling that life has been kind to him wants to give something of himself back to life."[16] I strongly advise working mothers, especially if their children are infants, to quit their jobs. They should have no fear of depriving their infants of some material benefits when they can give themselves instead. I hold a special place in my heart for handicapped and retarded children. I believe that they, even more than nonhandicapped children, need a mother's unconditional love and acceptance to prepare them for what they will face when they go to school.

Hospitalized Infants

Another group who especially need their mothers are hospitalized children. Studies have shown that young children whose mothers don't spend a lot of time with them in the hospital have a significantly higher mortality rate.[17]

Over-indulgence Versus Deprivation

Don't forget that meeting an infant's desires can be either overdone or underdone. Overly-indulged infants become inappropriately optimistic and expect the world to look out for them when they reach adulthood. By contrast, deprived infants have a deep-seated pessimism, become hostile and resentful when their needs are not met, and tend to give up easily.[18]

Harlow's Monkeys

Harry and Margaret Harlow, a husband and wife research team, have conducted a well-known study on
mother substitution with monkeys. They removed young
monkeys from their mothers and put them in areas where
they could choose between two imitation mothers. One
"mother" was made out of wire, and had a baby bottle
attached that was kept full of milk. The other "mother"
was a soft, terry cloth mother, but with no feeding device
attached. Interestingly, the monkeys would get milk from
the wire mother but ran to the soft terry cloth mother
whenever they were frightened. [19] This experiment clearly
applies to the human scene. Mothers who give love and
warmth are essential.

What About Day-care Centers?

Even more so than during infancy, mother substitutes
through the toddler years present a serious problem. Any
prolonged separation from the mother during this stage
can result in a loss of initiative or even the determination
for survival. Many children in America today are being
farmed out to day-care centers, many of which are detrimental to the child's eventual mental health and outlook
on life. Those day-care centers that are worthwhile, have
adequate staff and programming, and are somewhat beneficial to the child, are usually so expensive that it doesn't
pay for the mother to work. An adequate day-care center
should have at least one well-adjusted, warm, loving staff
member for every three or four toddlers.

Mary Curtis Blehar, in an excellent, in depth piece of
research, makes the following observations:

> Twenty two and three-year old children attending
> full time group day-care were compared with twenty

home-reared children of the same ages in a standardized situation. Analysis focused on responses to separation from and reunion with the mother. Findings indicated qualitative disturbances in the mother-child relationship in day-care children, and this was attributed to the disruptive effects of frequent daily separations. The child's age at the time that day-care began influenced the kind of disturbance shown. Those who started day-care at age two showed avoidant behavior upon reunion with the mother, whereas those who started day-care at age three showed anxious, ambivalent behavior.

The findings demonstrated that day-care children of both ages interacted less with their mothers than did home-reared children. During separation they cried more and showed more oral behavior and avoidance of the stranger. Upon reunion with the mother, they exhibited more avoidant and resistant behaviors.

The finding of anxious, ambivalent attachment behavior in the older day-care children and avoidant behavior in the younger day-care children is consistent with age differences reported in children's responses to major separation. During major separation, it is also the younger children (age 1–2¼) who are more likely to become detached and respond to the mother with indifference upon reunion, whereas the older children (age 3–4) are less likely to consolidate detachment and more likely to respond to reunion with the mother in an anxious ambivalent fashion. *Thus, the results of the present study suggest that many repetitions of minor separation may have effects similar in form (although not in severity) to major separations.* [20]

The Childhood of 714 Prisoners

In 1965, distinguished London psychiatrists studied the backgrounds of 546 female prisoners and 168 male prisoners. They concluded that the main factors contributing to the eventual delinquency of the prisoners were "multiplicity of care and lack of stable parent figures in childhood."[21] Also, many prisoners, during their early childhood, had experienced the loss of one or both parents through death.

Parent Substitutes

Ideally, toddlers should have their mothers home with them during the day, and interact with both parents on evenings and weekends. They should also have opportunity under parental supervision to interact with other children their own age, such as in Sunday school or with neighbors. The climbing divorce rate in America is separating more children from their fathers, and, in most cases, mothers are forced by economics to go to work, therefore depriving their children of a stable relationship with them. When a death occurs in the family, especially if the young toddler loses one or both of his parents, then it's time for grandparents, other close relatives, or close friends to step in and help the toddler reestablish a close maternal- or parental-child relationship as soon as possible, even if the close relative or friend involved doesn't live in the same house. Children need two parents—that's all there is to it! If I die while my children are still growing up, I certainly hope that my wife will get married again, to a stable, Christian man—and the sooner the better. The apostle Paul advised, "so I counsel younger widows to marry, to have children, to manage their homes, and to give the enemy no opportunity for slander" (1 Tim. 5:14).

Six Million Fatherless in Single-Parent Families

Another crucial problem in American society is the increasing number of single-parent families. They have problems all their own, such as separation, anxiety, grief, anger, depression, and loneliness, along with sexual identity problems in their children.[22] More than six million children in the United States are living in fatherless homes. An extensive study on 120 children from fatherless homes was presented by the psychiatry department of the University of Florida.[23] They found out that parent-child relationships are most seriously impaired among "hardcore" fatherless children—those who have been without a father for two years or more. Most of these children are either psychotic or retarded, with severe pathology and a fatalistic view of life. Children without a father for less than two years have fewer severe impairments than the "hardcore" fatherless, but more problems than children who have fathers. What a challenge to responsible fatherhood! Christian fathers who fail in their responsibilities before God are a heavy burden on my heart. It cannot be over-emphasized that a father's first responsibility before God is his own family. All else comes in a distant second. Paul said that if anyone does not provide for the needs of his own household, he is "worse than an unbeliever" (I Tim. 5:8). Boys in their preschool years whose fathers have been gone for an extended time have expressed more antisocial behavior later.[24]

Obesity in Childhood

One of the world's leading authorities on anorexia (loss of appetite) and obesity problems is Hilda Bruch, a prominent woman physician. From her research she notes that women who feel a conscious or unconscious rejection of their children frequently compensate by excessively feeding and overprotecting them. For them, food has an exaggerated emotional value and becomes a love-substitute. She also notes that frequently these mothers are frustrated career women who don't respect their husbands.[25]

Where Do We Go from Here?

Harold Voth candidly challenges America's parents:

> If young women are to be increasingly drawn into the working world through a change in social values, then who will provide care for the children many of these women will have? Making a family and caring for children

is a full-time career which only the most mature should accept. Society will pay an extremely high price if the enormous importance of child care by parents in a home is downgraded or lost sight of. Ever increasing numbers of children will eventually swell the ranks of emotionally disturbed adults. It has been estimated that ten to thirty million children are in need of psychiatric help. Suicide has become the second leading cause of death in the young. Deprive the child of a happy home life and you deprive him of his mental health (p. 207). . . . One of the outstanding women of psychiatry and psychoanalysis, Helene Deutsch, has written a painfully frank account of her past life under the heading of "Confrontations with myself." She now freely admits that she deprived her son and herself of a rich source of happiness by not devoting herself full-time to his care. She attributes her ability to have done so to her own unconscious conflicts which consisted of her deep identification with her father, her envy of the male, and her profound hostility toward her mother; and, also, to the pressures of her career. Her mother had dominated family life, including Dr. Deutschs' father, whom she describes as a passive man. She believes motherhood is a full-time occupation, and she regrets not having followed her own good judgment at the time."[26]

From the evidence presented in this chapter, the dangers of substitute child-care should be obvious to all but the most naive. Our society has been duped. Our government has been mislead. Relegating child care to day-care centers or to the government could become our nation's downfall. It will keep psychiatrists swamped with business. But most psychiatrists I know, including myself, would rather be forced into another field of medicine by a major trend back to mental health. We do not look forward to an increased load of counseling therapy left by the rampant breakdown of the family.

A Personal Experience

As a psychiatrist, I have extensively read studies on the psychological damage on children from experiences in day-care centers. But, I never felt the full impact of those studies until this personal experience with one. My wife and I had some shopping to do together, and our usual babysitter was not available. As a last resort, we left our son at a reputable neighborhood day-care center for about four hours. Feeling hurried, we failed to look past the waiting room until we came to pick up our son. The day-care people couldn't find him, so they allowed us in the children's area to see if we recognized him. We were appalled when we saw minibunk recesses, almost like cages, along the walls. Some children were playing with toys on the floor, but most were sitting in their "cages," staring out at me. They looked sad and lonely, and it was obvious that many of them were used to reporting to their "cages" daily. We didn't find our two-year-old son, so we frantically looked outside. He had wandered out of the day-care center unnoticed, and we found him playing in a nearby parking lot with cars driving back and forth near him. My wife and I were thankful that he was alive. We have never used a day-care center since, although we have used high-quality nursery schools for "half-day breaks."

Paul Meier, M.D.

Notes

1. Theodore Lidz, *The Person* (New York: Basic Books, 1968), p. 117.

2. Ibid.

3. Mohsen Ziai, ed., *Pediatrics* (Boston: Little, Brown and Company, n.d.), p. 48.

4. Gary Collins, *Man in Transition: The Psychology of Human Development* (Carol Stream, Ill.: Creation House, 1971), p. 39.

5. Rene A. Spitz, "Hospitalism: An Inquiry into the Genesis of Psychiatric Conditions in Early Childhood," in *The Psychoanalytic Study of the Child*, ed. Ruth S. Eissler et al., 25 vols. (New York: International Universities Press, 1945), 1:53–74.

6. Sue L. Evans, John B. Reinhart, and Ruth A. Succop, "Failure to Thrive: A Study of 45 Children and Their Families," *Journal of the American Academy of Child Psychology* 11 (1972): 440–457.

7. R. Melzack, "The Role of Early Experience in Emotional Arousal," *Annals of the New York Academy of Science* 159 (1969): 721.

8. G. F. Soloman, "Emotions, Stress, the Central Nervous System and Immunity," *Annals of the New York Academy of Science* 159 (1969): 7.

9. P. S. Goldman, "The Relationship Between the Amount of Stimulation in Infancy and Subsequent Emotionality," *Annals of the New York Academy of Science* 159 (1969): 640–650.

10. I. C. Kaufman, et al., "Effects of Separation from Mother on Emotional Behavior of Infant Monkeys," *Annals of the New York Academy of Science* 159 (1969): 681–695.

11. Ibid.

12. John Peters, *Lectures on Piaget* (Little Rock: University of Arkansas Child Study Center, 1973).

13. Eugene McDanald, "Emotional Growth of the Child," *Texas Medicine* 63 (1967): 74.

14. Ibid.

15. Ibid.

16. Ibid., p. 79.

17. Lidz, *The Person*, p. 150. See also M. D. Lynch and C. Ounsted, "Family Unit in Children's Psychiatric Hospital," *British Medical Journal* 2 (1975). 127–129.

18. Lidz, *The Person*, p. 151.

19. Harry F. Harlow and Margaret K. Harlow, *The Affectional Systems in Behavior of Non-Human Primates*, ed. A. M. Schrier et al., vol. 2 (New York: Academic Press, 1965).

20. Mary Curtis Blehar, "Anxious Attachment and Defensive Reactions Associated With Day Care," *Child Development* 45 (1974): 691.

21. F. Brown et al., "Childhood Bereavement and Subsequent Crime," *British Journal of Psychiatry* 112 (1966): 1048.

22. Robert Krell, "Problems of the Single-Parent Family Unit," *Canadian Medical Association Journal* 107 (1972): 867–868.

23. Joan L. Kogelschatz, Paul L. Adams, and Daniel Tucker, "Family Styles of Fatherless Households," *Journal of the American Academy of Child Psychiatry* 11 (1972): 356–383.

24. Boyd R. McCandless, *Children: Behavior and Development* (New York: Holt, Rinehart and Winston, 1967), p. 173.

25. Hilda Bruch, "Family Transactions in Eating Disorders," *Comprehensive Psychiatry* 12 (1972): 238–248.

26. Harold Voth, *The Castrated Family* (Mission, Kan.: Sheed Andrews and McMeel, 1977), p. 193.

4

What You Don't Know Will Hurt Your Children

Practically everyone is for day-care, but practically all the evidence says it's bad for preschoolers in all but its most costly forms. Most people do not know that psychologists and psychiatrists have grave misgivings about the concept because of its potential effects on personality; nor do they know that the officials of countries that have had considerable experience with day care are now warning of its harmful effects on children.[1]

After 150 hours of researching the evidence, I agree that many leading psychiatrists and sociologists in our country do indeed warn about the harmful effects of day-care centers. Experts agree on these two factors: (1) the most crucial time in the development of a person's emotional and intellectual potential is in his first five years of life, and (2) the most vital ingredient during that most important time is the mother-child relationship.

Frankly, the research depressed me. I found myself anxious to get back to my boys because the evidence convinced me of my need to spend more time with them (and that was while they were being cared for by a grandparent.) One day I broke into tears while sitting in the medical library. I was reading an account of the stages a little boy went through while being left at a hospital nursery for nine days. "John" even had psychological problems three years later, as they observed in a follow-up study. Here are some excerpts from his case study:

> ... Fifth day: constant misery attracted some attention from the nurses, but they could not comfort him or interest him in toys. He ate nothing all day. As no nurses had direct responsibility for him their concern was dispersed and ineffectual. His face and his eyes were swollen. He cried in quiet despair, sometimes rolling about and wringing his hands. Occasionally he shouted angrily at no one in particular. John now made fewer direct approaches to the nurses ... he turned to a teddy bear that was larger than himself. While the other children were rushing about or clamoring over the young nurses, John would sit somewhere burrowed into the teddy bear.

> ... Sixth Day: John was miserable and inactive. When nurse Mary was on duty, her face registered concern for him, but the system of group care frustrated them both and her concern was lost in the babel of the other toddlers. John's mouth trembled with tears held in check. In contrast to the beginning of his stay when he stood out as the brightest and the bonniest of the children, he was now unhappy and forlorn.

> ... Seventh Day: John cried weakly but continually all day. He did not play, he did not eat, did not make demands, and did not respond to the young nurses who attempted to cheer him. He stumbled as he walked. He was unhappy and he whimpered. His expression was dull and blank.

> ... Eighth Day: John was even more miserable and inactive. There was an angry note to his cries ... there was no respite to his unhappiness. For long times he lay in apathy on the floor, his head on the large teddy bear, impassive when other children came to him. He still ate little. When John's father came at tea time and tried to help, John was so distraught that he could neither eat nor drink. He cried convulsively over his cup. At the end of the visit, John abandoned to despair, and no one could comfort him, not even his favorite nurse, Mary. When she tried to take him on her knee, he squirmed down to the floor and crawled into a corner beside the teddy bear. There he lay crying, completely unresponsive to the troubled nurse.

... Ninth Day: John cried from the moment he awoke, hanging over his cot and shaking with sobs. In the discussion with nursery staff afterwards, they agreed among themselves that *"We have had many children like John."*[2]

Bear in mind that John was not mistreated in the least. His main problem was the "system," which had a multiplicity of caretakers.

Many women in this country have been mislead. I recently saw a "public service announcement" on television that totally unnerved me. Lasting about ninety seconds, the gist of it was: "Leave your child in a day-care facility . . . it's *good* for your *child*." That is a lie!

You may be familiar with the tale "The Emperor's New Clothes," but if not, I will briefly relate the story.

For an important occasion the Emperor wanted a most splendid outfit to wear. He instructed the royal tailors to make exquisite apparel for him. When he tried on the assorted clothes that the royal tailors had made, none of them pleased him at all. The tailors together decided to present a "pretend" outfit to him and act as if it were the most splendid outfit that they had ever seen.

When they presented the Emperor with this imaginary outfit, they "oohed" and "aahed" at how marvelously well it looked on him. Although the Emperor never saw the outfit, he felt he would appear stupid if he didn't acknowledge this garment that everybody else thought was so splendid looking. He actually bought it and "wore" it through the city as he was being greeted by the townspeople.

As he paraded down the main street, everybody shouted, "Look at the Emperor's new clothes!" Although nobody actually saw anything other than the Emperor's underwear, they all thought that everybody else could! This charade continued until, finally, a little boy, undaunted by what he was hearing, noticed that the ruler wasn't wearing any outer clothing and said, "Look! The Emperor isn't wearing anything!" At that point, the Emperor became very embarrassed, standing in front of the people in only his underwear.

Likewise, more and more people are saying, "Look at how great day care is!" "Look how good it is for the little ones!" "Look how rewarding it is to be an employed mother!" Those who do not go along with this philosophy are made to feel like they must be wrong. I've done the research, and I've looked at the facts. I'm going to say, as the little boy said, "This is what I see." Perhaps you, too, will have the courage to admit something you see no matter what others are shouting.

Fact One: Most Day Care Facilities Are Inadequate

Mary Dublin Kerserling shares this conclusion based on research done by the National Council of Jewish Women:

> The larger part is a composite picture of much care that is only custodial, some that is bad, and far too much that is harmful. A part of the story is that far too many children get no care at all.[3]

Researchers visited 431 centers in which nearly 24,000 children were enrolled. Only 1 percent of the proprietary centers and 9 percent of the nonprofit centers observed provided "truly developmental care."[4]

Ms. magazine reported:

> Since most for-profit centers do not enroll federally subsidized children, they are governed only by the state licensing codes. These state laws are designed to protect only a child's health and safety. Depending on the state, they allow 10 to 20 children to be cared for by one teacher or staff member.[5]

After surveying about forty-five day-care centers in Atlanta, the Council of Jewish Women concluded that "the physical facilities are unbelievably inadequate, crowded, dark, with poor or no playgrounds."[6]

An article, "Dilemma for Working Mothers," mentioned that some day-care facilities are saving money by cutting to a minimum such services as counseling, education, and even meals. Some ignore state licensing laws by enrolling more children and hiring fewer staff members than regulations allow. The same article cites the Child Welfare League estimate that 77 percent of available child-care spaces are inadequate and should not be used at all. "Experts say they have the effect of reducing day-care centers to warehouses, where children are simply stored."[7]

The *Washington Monthly* states:

> Most (day-care facilities) do not meet the widely accepted standards of 'quality' because the government has never enforced the standards it adopted in 1968. Recent study by HEW of 607 federally funded day-care centers in 9 different states found that 70 percent failed to meet federal standards of health and safety and that children's lives were actually endangered in some of them.[8]

Even if one was uncertain about the detrimental effects that a good day-care situation might afford, experts agree that anything but quality day-care is *clearly damaging to the child.*

Fact Two: Your Child May Be Receiving Improper Care

Because most day-care centers pay the minimum wage, it is difficult to attract and retain professionally trained personnel. "With salaries so low as was to be expected, the majority of the staff were people with little or no training in early childhood education or development."[9]

Not only are many of the personnel simply unqualified, but also since they are not required to take a psychological profile before working, it is possible that some of the workers are emotionally unstable.

After observing the quality of care in forty-five centers in Atlanta, the Council of Jewish Women reached this conclusion concerning the handling of the children:

> ... even worse, the concern for the child—the individual development of each—is all but totally lacking. Concern is almost completely custodial and disciplined. We have concluded that since serious damage can be done by poor day care, in many cases no care is better. [10]

But the central problem with day-care situations goes beyond the poor facilities, the poor adult-child ratio, or even the lack of professionally trained personnel. It is the system itself. What harms children most is the multiplicity of caretakers. That is, no particular adult is assigned to two or three children. Instead, all the children are the wards of all the caretakers. Therefore, an intimate (one-to-one) relationship is seldom established between a child and a caring, mother-substitute.

> A multiplicity of mother figures is often accompanied by insufficient adult-child interaction. In most institutions where each child, in the course of a day, has many caretakers, each adult has partial responsibility for many children. Under these circumstances two factors combine to give insufficiency of interaction: no adult has time to give much attention to any one child and, since no adult is familiar with the particular behavior of each child, many of the children's social signals go unheeded. [11]

An adequate day-care situation specifically assigns each adult to no more than three or four children. But even with this provision, problems can arise.

First, the turnover of staff is generally high. "Since more often than not, physical facilities are downright depressing and salaries simply ridiculous... it is not surprising that a rapid turnover of staff is the rule rather than the exception." [12]

Second, not only is the staff likely to change, but also it

has been found that many children are frequently transferred to other day-care situations. One study showed that approximately 25 percent of children under three and 34 percent of those between three and six years had experienced four or more day-care arrangements.[13] Therefore, even if some children do establish good, close relationships with other adults, many are likely to "suffer" another "separation" either when their caretakers change jobs or when the children themselves are transferred to other centers. In using the words "inadequate care," I am not referring to custodial care. Most day-care situations will keep children physically safe. I am referring instead to the emotional welfare of the child. Emotional needs frequently go unheeded, as revealed in the following quote:

> In ordinary life (family life) there is always some awareness of the changing needs and moods of a younger member. There is a measure of certainty that unhappiness, hunger, tiredness and playfulness will be answered more or less appropriately and without too much delay.
>
> For the young child in the family, there are some known and expected responses because the same one or two people will be tending to him. Even if his first cry is not taken too seriously, a real need is unlikely to go unanswered. Not so in the majority of institutions with their changing caretakers.
>
> These respond in varying ways to what they see, *if* and *when* they see it. They are unlikely to see, or understand, the subtleties of the new child's gestures, language, needs and anxieties. *Just when he most needs to be understood, protected, reassured, he is most likely to be overlooked or handled without empathy and understanding.* Several strange people will deal with him, one after another, and no one of them will share his anxieties, or support him through the maze of new experiences.[14]

Fact Three: "Basic Trust" in Your Child's Personality Is Developed in the First Years of Life (Especially His First Year)

An infant establishes this "basic trust" during the first few months of life. During this time the baby senses that his mother and the few others who are meeting his needs (father, sister, or grandparent) can be trusted and will not desert him. "If there are too many different caretakers, or too frequent changes in caretakers, the baby's fear of being left alone interferes with normal development.[15]

Fact Four: Your Child May Suffer Some Degree of Loss of Identity

Most psychiatrists believe that an infant kept all day in a large day-care center will be unable to develop a sufficient intensity in its relationship with its mother figure. Consequently, the infant will compensate by developing an unusually strong attachment to other children in the nursery, which can result in a loss of strong individual identity.[16]

Because these "children form unusually strong attachments to their peer groups,"[17] they are likely also to experience undue peer pressure.

Fact Five: Peer Pressure Stifles a Child's Individualism

Toddlers in day-care centers face peer pressure prematurely. It is difficult enough to face it later in adolescence. Even adults don't always cope with peer pressure successfully.

In studying adolescents and adults raised in a group nursery at Kibbutz Bettleheim in Israel, experts found that those individuals tended to conform too quickly to group pressures. The results of the kibbutz scholastic tests made "eerie reading." The tests revealed that almost none of the kibbutz children scored either in the lower range of the scale or in the upper range (unlike any other comparable group of children). Because their scores were clustered at the middle, it was concluded that, "While the kibbutz nurseries have succeeded in eliminating the underachiever, they also have eliminated the scholar, the artist, and the leader."[18]

Every society needs individuals who excel in the various fields, from science to art. No wonder the Hungarian government presently is moving away from day-care, and now pays directly to the mother a day-care allowance for each child.[19]

> Kremlinologists [those who study the policies of the Soviet Union] have noticed an astounding reversal by the government, from praise for their fifty-year-old day-care system to concern over the possibility that day care causes "deprivation of psychological stimulation" and "one-sided or retarded development".... The Soviet authorities now realize that they have been producing some drones with their group care in the first two or three years.[20]

Fact Six: "Affectionless Character" May Result from Mother-Child Separation

Early studies emphasize what John Bowlby terms "affectionless character," which is the impairment of the capacity to form and maintain deep and lasting relationships.[21]

Interestingly, many studies of childhood and adolescent backgrounds of criminals revealed either a complete lack of or poor mother-child relationships. The "affectionless character" from inadequate maternal care is most likely the primary factor causing the capacity in criminals to commit atrocious crimes seemingly with no conscience whatsoever about these acts.

"Affectionless character" also adversely affects adults in their marriage relationships. "In studying adolescents and adults who had been raised in Kibbutz Bettleheim it was found that they had great difficulty in forming strong personal relationships with others, even in marriage."[22]

Basically, adults brought up in day-care situations may readily make many friends, but only superficially. They would have a hard time becoming intimate and therefore are unable to commit themselves to individuals.

Fact Seven: Your Child's Social Behavior May Be Affected Now as Well as Later On in Life

Although "common sense" might prompt the assumption that children reared in day-care situations would respond more rapidly to strangers than those raised in home situations, it has been established that

> Day-care children are more avoidant of strangers than their home-raised peers ... this finding is congruent with those of Tizard and Tizard (1971), who found young children reared in residential nurseries to be more afraid of strangers than home-reared children, and those of Heincke and Westheimer (1965) who previously found separated children highly fearful of persons they had seen months before during separations.[23]

In observing children's social behavior with other children, it was found that "daily contact with other children didn't automatically increase socio-ability. In fact, at twenty-nine months, home-raised tots were a bit more sociable than day-care children."[24]

The most harm done socially to the child because of day care involves his relationships (interactions) with adults. In a study by Macrae and Jackson on nineteen pairs of four-year-olds using nine behavioral traits (the children matched in age, sex, race and had spent either a minimum of two years or just a few months in a day-care situation), it was suggested that "children who had been in the day-care center since infancy were less cooperative with adults, more physically and verbally agressive with adults and peers, and more motorically active than children who were relatively new to day care."[25]

These findings on children's cooperation with adults and their ability to get along with peers paralleled the results from other studies:

> Ralph, Thomas, Chess, and Korn (1968) reported that children with two years of nursery school had a higher percentage of negative interactions with teachers ... those who had experienced substitute care before age five were significantly more self-assertive, less conforming, less impressed by punishment.[26]

Fact Eight: The "Strange" Environment Can Be Hard on Your Child

Imagine what it must be like for a two-year-old in a new day-care situation. The toddler will be offered strange foods and given strange implements with which to eat. The child might be helped too little or too much. The noise and movement during mealtimes impose strain. And instead of toileting geared to the toddler's particular needs as happens at home, toileting will conform to the institution's routine. The child's special signs or calls will probably be undetected.

The schedule may be totally rearranged:

> The child used to sleeping for several hours in the morning and having a late lunch may find himself too tired to eat lunch, wakeful when others sleep, and ready for sleep just as the rest wake up. His sleeping rhythm will be disturbed.[27]

Considering how the noise and movement of group life are strenuous for an adult not accustomed to them, can you imagine how much more so it must be for a two-year-old struggling with so much confusion?

Fact Nine: Your Child Is More Subject to Communicable Diseases in a Day-Care Situation

Many of my friends who have children in a day-care arrangement complain of their child's "perennial cold." It doesn't surprise me. During the winter the chances of at least one child in the center having a cold are high. One report concluded that day-care centers are increasingly facilitating the spread of communicable diseases "among a population not previously at risk."

> Enteric infections, such as shigellosis and hepatitis, are especially common because of the inadequate personal hygiene of young, non-toilet trained children. In our investigation, we found for the first time epidemic giardiasis in day-care centers indicating that protozoa, like enteric bacteria and viruses, may be an important cause of illness in these institutions.[28]

Fact Ten: Immediate Emotional Effects Will Be Characterized by Different "Symptoms"

The immediate effects include:

> (a) *protest*—characteristic by crying and acute distress at the loss of mother and by efforts to recapture her through the limited means at the child's disposal; (b) *despair*—characteristic by increasing hopelessness, withdrawal, and decreasing efforts to regain mother, for whom the child is mourning; and (c) *detachment*—characteristic by 'settling down' in the separation environment, accepting the care of whatever substitute figures are available, but with marked loss of attachment behavior to the mother when she returns. In subsequent reunion—clinging, crying for attention.[29]

One study mentioned that children frequently ignore their parents when they are reunited. This is their subconscious way of punishing their parents for having left them.

I shared these findings with a good friend, a nurse-practitioner who was, at the time, employed at a clinic where she both diagnosed and prescribed treatment. She loved her job and found her profession fulfilling. Her son was in the care of his own grandmother. Yet, with all this going for her, she was shocked that her son's behavior matched the symptoms of children in day-care centers. She responded, "I can't believe it! That's just how Chad acts!" She then started working three days a week instead of five. With the birth of her second child, she gave up her job completely. Although she misses her work, she feels that her children are worth the sacrifice she's making.

Bowlby also points out that children who experience "partial deprivation" have an "excessive" need for love. This was demonstrated clearly by what happened to Janet's (see first chapter) little girl Ginny. I first saw Ginny in our church nursery. Her mother had returned to work six months earlier. Ginny came to me immediately and sat on my lap and wanted me to hold her constantly. "Don't mind her," the regular worker said, "She just wants to be held all the time. She's always that way." Ginny *needed* to be held and loved. I hope that her day care worker was more understanding than the church worker was.

The ill effects of deprivation may be variously expressed or repressed by the child. Bowlby, who researched this area extensively, concludes:

> Partial deprivation brings in its train anxiety, excessive need for love, powerful feelings of revenge, and, arising from these last, guilt and depression. A young child cannot cope with all these emotions and drives. The ways in which he responds to these disturbances of his inner life may in the end bring about nervous disorders and instability of character.[30]

Certainly at least one (and probably more) of these areas in a deprived child's life will be affected. The "risks" of day-care are too eminent. The "price" is too high. It may cost both you and your child a lifetime of misery.

If you have placed your child in day-care, you might be tempted to say, "Well, my child was in a day-care center the first four years of life and certainly turned out fine." My answer is that your child would probably be even better off if he had been kept at home with you. Regardless of how "good" your child turns out to be, my opinion is that your child would be more emotionally stable and happier without the experience in a day-care situation.

Linda Burnett

Psychiatric Comment

Substitute mothering is not merely a twentieth-century development. It has been practiced for thousands of years, from the time of baby Moses. In 1891, it was a topic of concern for M. E. Sangster, who wrote on the subject of babies' rights:

> ... Still, no matter how apparently worthy of trust a nurse or servant may be, unless she has been tried and proved by long and faithful service and friendship, a babe is too precious to be given unreservedly to her care. The mother herself, or an elder sister or auntie, should hover protectingly near the tiny creature, whose lifelong happiness may depend on the way its babyhood is passed. Who has not seen in the city parks the beautifully dressed infants, darlings evidently of homes of wealth and refinement, left to bear the beams of the sun and stings of gnats and flies, while the nurses gossip together, oblivious of the flight of time? Mothers are often quick to resent stories of the neglect or cruelty of their employees, and cannot be made to believe that their own children are sufferers. And the children are too young to speak.
>
> The lover of little ones can almost always see the subtle difference which exists between infants cared for by their own mothers and the babies who are left to hirelings. The former have a sweeter, shyer, gladder look than the latter. Perhaps the babies who are born, so to speak, with silver spoons in their mouths, are better off than those who came to the heritage of a gold spoon. The gold spooners have lovely cradles and bassinets. They wear valenciennes, lace and embroidery, and the fashion dictates the cut of their bibs, and the length of their flowing robes. They are waited upon by bonnes in picturesque aprons and caps, and the

doctor is sent for whenever they have the colic. The little silver spooners, on the other hand, are arrayed in simple slips, which the mother made herself in dear delicious hours, the sweetest in their mystic joy which happy womanhood knows. They lie on the sofa, or on two chairs with a pillow placed carefully to hold them, while she sings at her work, spreads the snowy linen on the grass, moulds the bread, and shells the peas. The mothers' hands wash and dress them, the father rocks them to sleep, the proud brothers and sisters carry them to walk, or wheel their little wagons along the pavement. Fortunate babies of the silver spoon.[31]

Paul Meier, M.D.

Notes

1. Marjorie Boyd, "The Case Against Day Care," *The Washington Monthly,* 1976, p. 22.

2. James and Joyce Robertson, "Young Children in Brief Separation," in *The Psychoanalytic Study of the Child,* ed. Ruth S. Eissler, vols. 26–33 (New Haven: Yale University Press, 1974), 26: 264–315.

3. Mary Dublin Kerserling, "A Report Based on Findings of the National Council of Jewish Women," *Windows on Day-Care* (New York: National Council of Jewish Women), p. 10.

4. Ibid., p. 4.

5. Joyce Goldman, "Vacuum Packed Day Care," *Ms,* March 1975, p. 81.

6. Kerserling, "A Report," p. 11.

7. *U.S. News & World Report,* 12 April 1976, pp. 49–50.

8. Boyd, "Case Against Day Care," p. 22.

9. Kerserling, "A Report," p. 12.

10. Ibid., p. 20.

11. John Bowlby, *Child Care and the Growth of Love* (Baltimore: Penguin Books, 1965), p. 48.

12. Joan L. Bergstrom and Jane R. Gold, "Day Care and Child Development," *Sweden's Day Nurseries: Focus on Programs for Infants and Toddlers* (Mt. Rainer, Maryland: Daycare and Child Development Council of America, Inc., n.d.).

13. Greta G. Fein and Alison Clarke-Stewart, *Day Care in Context* (New York: John Wiley & Sons, 1973), p. 43.

14. Robertson, "Young Children in Brief Separation," p. 327.

15. Boyd, "Case Against Day Care," p. 22.

16. Ibid.

17. Ibid.

18. Ibid., p. 28.

19. Ibid.

20. Ibid.

21. Bowlby, *Child Care*, p. 215.

22. Boyd, "Case Against Day Care," p. 22.

23. Mary Curtis Blehar, "Anxious Attachment and Defensive Reactions Associated with Day-Care," *Child Development* 45 (1974): 691.

24. Jerome Kagan, "Day Care Is As Good As Home Care," *Psychology Today*, May 1976.

25. John W. Macrae and Emily Herbert Jackson, "Are Behavior Effects of Infant Day Care Programs Specific?" *Developmental Psychology* 12 (May 1976): 269–270.

26. J. C. Schwartz, R. Strickland, and G. Krolic, "Infant Day Care: Behavioral Effects at Preschool Age," *Developmental Psychology* 10 (July 1974): 504.

27. Robertson, "Young Children in Brief Separation," pp. 264–315.

28. R. E. Black, et al., "Giardiasis in Day-Care Centers: Evidence of Person to Person Transmission," *Pediatrics* 60 (October 1977): 486–491.

29. Bowlby, *Child Care*, p. 14.

30. Ibid.

31. M. E. Sangster, "Babies and Their Rights," in *Fireside Fancies*, ed. Annie R. White (1891).

5

A Biblical View of Child-Rearing

The rod of correction imparts wisdom, but a child left to itself disgraces his mother (Prov. 29:15).

Discipline your son and he will give you peace; he will bring delight to your soul (Prov. 29:17).

Our children *need* to be corrected. This is how we train up our children in the way that they should go (cf. Prov. 22:6). By persistently encouraging good behavior and disciplining bad behavior, we help shape their characters. But the key is a repeated and consistent interrelationship with our children. Each action a child makes either begins a new habit or strengthens an old one. In this context, every action is consequential.

God said through Moses:

These commandments that I give you today are to be upon your hearts. Impress them on your children. Talk about them when you sit at home and when you walk along the road, when you lie down and when you get up (Deut. 6:6,7).

No way can we teach our children while sitting in the house, out taking a walk, or after nap time, *unless they are with us.* It is significant that these various times and activities are mentioned in this biblical passage. How important repetition is! Our children are to learn about God almost daily and in every situation because in every situation they *are* learning something.

I frequently hear the words, "It's not the quantity of time I spend with my children that counts, it's the quality." But this statement is inaccurate. Unless we spend a quantity of time with our children, the "quality" times may never happen. The times we least expect to be special with our children later end up "bowling us over" with meaning when we reflect upon them. And what about the lack of quality time they may be experiencing away from their parents.

Long before psychiatrists and sociologists discovered how significant the first few years of life are, God admonished us that if we train up a child in the way that he should go, when he is old he will not depart from it (cf. Prov. 22:6). This means that the character formed during childhood will be the same character continued through adulthood. Henry Brandt, a well-known psychologist, made this statement concerning parenthood: "Parenthood is the process of making disciples of your children."[1]

God said through the prophet, "Who is it he is trying to teach? To whom is he explaining his message? To children weaned from their milk, to those just taken from the breast? For it is: Do and do, do and do, rule on rule, rule on rule; a little here, a little there" (Isa. 28:9, 10). This implies that it takes *time* to nurture our children in the love and discipline of the Lord. "Teachable moments" happen throughout each day, usually prompted by a child's natural curiosity: "Mommy, why do people die? Where did they go?" How would a non-Christian answer that for your child? The answers children receive will go into their memory banks to permanently shape their conscious and subconscious beliefs, forming the fabric of their adult convictions. Or an incident could occur from which they could learn. Would a non-Christian respond to a frustrating moment the same as a Christ-controlled mother? Or will your children learn impatience and cursing? "My day-care worker *is* a Christian," you may claim. What if she's busy with someone else's child when your child's "teachable moment" comes up?

Moses wrote, "*When* your son *asks* you [teachable moment]... say to him, 'With a mighty hand the Lord brought us out of Egypt, out of the land of slavery" (Exod. 13:14). How much more impact our teaching will have if we are, as parents, sufficiently available to answer our children's spontaneous questions. With this in mind, a day-care center is a *powerful* teaching situation. A day-care program that has a child from six months to six years has over 8,000 hours to teach that child *values, fear, beliefs,* and *behaviors.*[2]

Not only time, but *repetition* as well is needed to train up our children. Notice "Do and do, do and do, rule on rule, rule on rule" (Isa. 28:10) Consistency is supremely important. Something that was wrong yesterday is wrong today. Something that required discipline last week should be disciplined this week as well.

According to God's Word, parents' love is demonstrated by disciplining their children. "He who spares the rod hates his son: but he who loves him is careful to discipline him" (Prov. 13:24). Their whole lives will be dependent, to a large degree, on the way they were "trained up." If our children, while they're young and flexible, do not learn obedience to their earthly parents, how can we believe that they will be nonresistant to God's commands when they are adults? "Discipline your son, for in that there *is hope;* do not be a willing party to his death" (Prov. 19:18).

"Folly is bound up in the heart of a child; but the rod of discipline will drive it far from him" (Prov. 22:15). The Bible's use of the word *folly* or *foolishness,* is not what we usually think—like silly, nonsensical, or lighthearted. Where folly or foolishness is mentioned in the Bible, the connotation is much more serious and implies spiritual and emotional immaturity and depravity. For example: "The fool says in his heart, 'There is no God'" (Ps. 14:1); "foolish people have reviled your name" (Ps. 74:18): "Some became fools through their rebellious ways and suffered affliction because of their iniquities" (Ps. 107:17); "The fear of the Lord is the beginning of knowledge, but fools despise wisdom and discipline" (Prov. 1:7); and "He who conceals his hatred has lying lips, and whoever spreads slander is a fool" (Prov. 10:18).

Common sense may tell you that children will "grow out of" their foolishness, but this is not the case. Proverbs is full of instances of children growing up to be foolish adults, and their destiny is pitiful.

To illustrate, look at the woman who has not had the rod of correction drive out her foolishness when she was little: "The wise woman builds her house, but with her own hands the foolish one tears hers down" (Prov. 14:1).

The most significant consequences of parental neglect to "drive out the foolishness" affect both men and women in the development of their consciences, which are "maps" to help guide them in making *every* decision. The proverb "Fools mock at making amends for sin" (Prov. 14:9), indicates that such a person takes sin lightly—so lightly that fun is made of it. Have you ever noticed that many people who indulge in questionable activities laugh about them? Many even make fun of the "goody-goodies" who don't participate as they do.

I have a theory that children have a propensity toward God. We are told by Jesus, "Therefore, whoever humbles himself *like this child,* is greatest in the kingdom of God" (Matt. 18:4). Further, in reference to children, Jesus explains, "for the kingdom of Heaven belongs to such as they" (Matt. 19:14). Jesus commended a childlike faith.

As a teenager I went through a time of deep searching—a crucial, philosophical quest. "Why was I born?" "What is the meaning for my existence?" I praise God that I *found* meaning in the person of Jesus Christ. But I have noticed that many of my contemporaries also went through that phase as teenagers. The ones who didn't find Christ gradually stopped exploring the deeper questions of life and settled instead on the superficial, inconsequential aspects of living in this world for fulfilling their goals and discovering meaning.

While we're young, our soul's "ears" are more receptive to hearing God speak. As we get older, our "hearing" (conscience) may become gradually "cauterized," and what used to bother us doesn't mean much now.

> Vice is a monster of so frightful mien,
> As to be hated, needs but to be seen,
> Yet seen too oft, familiar with her face,
> We first endure, then pity, then embrace.
>
> *Alexander Pope*

An excellent analogy of this axiom is found in a scientist's experiment with a frog's adaptation to water temperature. At the beginning of the experiment he threw a live frog into boiling water. Of course, the frog jumped out immediately! Next, he placed the frog in lukewarm water. The frog liked the water and stayed in it. Gradually, in slight increments, the scientist increased the temperature, so that eventually the water started boiling. That frog was so used to the temperature, however, that it was boiled alive without even trying to jump out!

Just as that frog had come to a point of being comfortable in boiling water, so natural man, as he progresses in years, becomes more and more comfortable in activities that endanger his spiritual life.

This is not to say that God's grace can't be received by individuals past twelve years old. I became a Christian when I was eighteen. Through Christ I received a new conscience because I became a new creation (cf. 2 Cor. 5:17). I experienced the truth of the words, "How much more then, will the blood of Christ, who through the eternal Spirit offered himself unblemished to God, cleanse our consciences from the acts that lead to death, so that we may serve the living God" (Heb. 9:14).

But the conscience's capacity to "hear" may become weaker as the years go by. And the law of diminishing returns can apply—the sins that brought "kicks" before aren't enough now, so one needs to go one degree higher to get the same amount of kicks.

"A foolish son [brings] grief to his mother" (Prov. 10:1). As a mother, I don't know of anything that would break my heart more than to see any of my children grow up to be foolish by God's definition. In the biblical instruction on child-rearing, a central theme stands out: the consequences of how we train our children are permanent.

May Christian parents never forget the magnitude of their responsibility. And may they never forget God's promise that if they train their children in the way that they should go, they *will not depart from it!*

Linda Burnett

Psychiatric Comment

Many psychiatrists estimate on the basis of their studies that approximately 85 percent of the adult personality is already formed by the time the individual is six years old. Imagine that! A brand new baby, born in America today, may live to be seventy-five years old, and with new scientific discoveries, longevity may be extended to eighty-five or ninety. But how the parents train the baby during those crucial first six years will determine how that individual will enjoy and succeed in life during the other seventy or eighty years. God has given us parents a tremendous responsibility! The Communist Party has emphasized the importance of those early years. I believe that those of us in the evangelical community must also be aware of the important responsibility God has given those of us who have children, especially if they are under six years of age.

I would like to share one of God's warnings about chil-

dren that changed my whole outlook on the vast importance of child-rearing. This warning has given me more
determination in my work of family psychotherapy. This
warning also stirred up my desire to practice preventive
psychiatry, especially among my fellow Christians. That
crucial warning from God is: "For I, the Lord your God,
am a jealous God, punishing the children for the sin of the
fathers to the third and fourth generations of those who
hate me, but showing love to thousands who love me and
keep my commandments" (Exod. 20:5-6).

This passage troubled me when I first read it. I knew
that the Bible is without error, and yet I simply could not
understand how a loving God would punish three or four
generations of children for the sins of their parents. It
didn't seem consistent with those passages about Christ's
love for children as recorded in the Gospels. But when I
went into psychiatry and extensively studied about
healthy and unhealthy parent-child relationships, I saw
scores of mentally disturbed children and had to deal with
their parents and grandparents. Then the meaning of this
passage became obvious to me. It simply means that if
we, as parents, live sinful lives—lives that are not in ac-
cord with the health-producing principles of God's
Word—there will be a profound effect upon our children
and our children's children, to three or four generations.
God is not punishing our offspring for our sins; we
are—by not living according to his precepts.

In my review of scientific literature on parent-child relationships, and from my own experiences as a psychiatrist,
I have learned a great deal about which types of families
produce which types of mental illness in their children.
During one full year of research at Duke University, I also
uncovered ample information on which types of religious
backgrounds produce which types of mental illnesses, and
which types of religious experiences produce good mental
health.[3]

There are, however, exceptions to every rule. Some
children brought up under the most adverse circum-

stances attain greatness as adults. Others reared in relatively normal Christian homes develop manic-depression, schizophrenia, or some other mental illness because of a strong inherited predisposition or other factor. The human brain, with its forty billion cells, complicated biochemistry, and interconnecting circuits and electrical activity, is far too complex for us to be overly simplistic in our approach to mental illness. But, at the same time, there are definite trends that have been observed over and over again in the families of various types of mentally disturbed children.

Paul Meier, M.D.

Notes

1. Henry Brandt, "Insights for Loving" (Chuck Swindoll Radio Broadcast, Fullerton, Calif.)
2. Report to the President, *White House Conference on Children*, 1970, pp. 55–56.
3. The results of this study were integrated with 150 passages of Scripture related to various aspects of child-rearing in my book *Christian Child-Rearing and Personality Development* (Grand Rapids: Baker Book House, 1977), pp. 49–90. Also, the effects of various child-rearing practices on adult depression levels are treated in my second book, co-authored by Dr. Frank Minirth, *Happiness Is a Choice* (Grand Rapids: Baker Book House, 1978), pp. 43–107.

6

The Secular Threat
to the Family

My people perish for lack of knowledge.

What is happening to our country, and how are recent trends affecting us? Since societal changes are usually subtle and gradual, and therefore hardly detectable, look at what happened in another country. In *The Black Book of Red China*, under the chapter, "The Smashed Family System," the author writes:

> The complete breakdown of the family unit was necessary before the Party could be accepted as Big Brother or Father. . . . The party becomes a symbol of freedom of the sexes. Everything was condoned in relations between the sexes. Marriage is a matter of bedroom convenience . . . the offspring of such unions become conveniently the responsibility of the state. . . . The home naturally revolves around the child bearer. Using the issue of equality for women as a weapon, every artifice is employed to chisel away and destroy this feminine influence, whose biological and social needs stirred mankind into its quest for individual dignity and security. . . . The equality Communists talk of has its own meaning. The change in the status of Chinese women that resulted from this new marriage law gave heart-sickening evidence of it . . . Hitherto, they had certain privileges in

71

recognition of their natural differences as women . . . These are now being taken away from them . . . the equal rights accorded women put a man's wife and daughter alongside him in common bondage . . . Equality for women gave the man, too, the opportunity to toss aside his wife, simply by filling in a form declaring that she was ideologically incompatible . . . Significantly, since the new marriage law, suicide among women has risen to phenomenal heights . . . The relegation of a woman to the status of a cog in the same production mechanism as a man is what is presented to her as emancipation. This is a grotesque swindle. The communists had to attempt it for, while the woman retained her individual role, the family system could never be completely smashed. Peking realized full well that the survival of the family unit would be the Achilles heel of communism.[1]

Sound familiar?

Now, let's take a look at Sweden. Dr. Barbara Galewski observed:

The Swedish ERA has had economic, political and, above all, psychological effects which, unless one believes in conspiracies, I doubt anybody had forseen. It started as a more or less harmless feminist movement, building on the shame involved in being a housewife and mother— a parasite on society, as they called it, as contrasted to men and women who were equal soldiers in the same army. Swedish ERA friends had to declare housewives despicable before ERA could be introduced. The housewife sank low in appreciation . . . A small country of 8 million suddenly had to create about 400,000 new jobs for these "parasites" on a market that was already strained . . . Laws could be passed that employers had to employ 50% women, and the government industries all have at least 40% . . . while the laid off men go on welfare. But the real kiss of death came when men got equal option to take paternity leaves. Each expectant couple is allowed seven months compensated leave to be taken by either partner or split between the two. . . . Breaking down the family cell from being the most important part of society to a status of two sexless parents whose children are brought up by institutions while both parents work outside their home . . . ERA is the art of introducing something inferior to what you already have, while spending millions on it.[2]

The philosophy of many women behind the women's liberation movement is, by their own admission, anti-God and anti-Bible. Many of their leaders are humanists. What is humanism? The answer is found in the Humanist Manifesto of 1933, initiated by three Unitarian ministers in a revolt against orthodox Christianity. The Manifesto affirmed:

> Religious expression should be found in a heightened sense of personal life through search for joy in living rather than old attitudes of worship and prayer: there should be no uniquely religious emotions and attitudes of the kind hitherto associated with belief in the supernatural...

John Dewey, the father of progressive education, was primarily responsible for promoting humanism in America's schools. He was a signer of this document. In August of 1973, 120 religious leaders, philosophers, scientists, and educators signed Humanist Manifesto II, which justifies abortion, divorce, sexual freedom, euthanasia, and suicide. It rejects any religious moral code that "suppresses" freedom; says man must replace God; and urges the development of a world order. It states: "No deity will save us, we must save ourselves.... Promises of immortal salvation or fear of eternal damnation are both illusory and harmful...." The Manifesto goes on to affirm that "moral values derive their source from human experience. Ethics is autonomous" [do your own thing][3].

One of the byproducts of humanist philosophy was a concept of human behavior popularized as "situational ethics" or "values clarification." Advocates of situational ethics emphasize that human behavior and actions (whether considered traditionally as moral or immoral) are not to be judged by absolute standards of right or wrong (i.e., the seventh command forbidding adultery), but rather by the circumstances or situation that caused or motivated the particular behavior. For example, premarital sex can be justified if it reflects a "meaningful relationship"—one presumed to be motivated by love. Of course, in our society, love is an elastic concept that is stretched or twisted to justify practically any behavior that society formerly labeled as unlawful or immoral.

Situational ethics pervades TV programming, including prime time shows (i.e., "Dallas") that treat illicit sex casually. Extramarital affairs are portrayed frequently, at times depicted as the way out of a boring and unfulfilling marriage.

After a study based on 500 people monitoring television programming in 1978 and 1979, these sobering statistics were published: Viewers were exposed to 18,429 incidents of sex over a period of one year of prime time viewing. Sexual content within programs included explicit or implicit sexual intercourse, nudity or near-nudity, and explicit sexual comments. Nearly 87.5 percent of all sex shown on television was depicted outside of marriage. In 1979, over 68 percent of all prime time programs included sexual content. Nearly 53 percent of all prime time programs contained profanity.[4] Not only television, but magazines as well have declared the joys of open marriage and sexual freedom.

The epitome of what the women's movement is all about is revealed in what was recently observed as "International Women's Year." Conferences were held in all the states, with the National IWY Conference held in Houston, Texas, in November 1977. It was covered by TV several nights in a row. It gained a big spread in *Sports Illustrated*, among other magazines.

The purpose of these conferences, supposedly, was to afford an opportunity for every kind of woman, representing every viewpoint, to make a statement of her concern, and thereby showing the President and Congress what American women want *so that it could be used as a blueprint for future legislation.* "What women want" however, never was intended to be part of the IWY conference in the U.S. The Goals of IWY were written earlier, in June 1975, when the United Nations held its world conference of the International Women's Year in Mexico City, Mexico. It was there that the World Plan of Action for the Implementation of the Objectives of the International Women's Year was unanimously adopted. The World Plan did not set guidelines allowing American women to decide their own goals of IWY. Those goals were predetermined.

The state conferences, however, went as expected. But since there were so many negative reports, the U.S. government conducted special hearings to verify the complaints of illegal violations of fair representation. Senator Jessie A. Helms, who presided at the hearings, charged:

> Enough information has come to light to reveal a widespread pattern and practice of discrimination by IWY and its state affiliates against those who do not agree with the narrow and negative ideology and partisan biases of IWY organizers. . . . Reports indicate rigged sessions, handpicked committees, stacked registration, and little or no publicity to women at large . . . The IWY program represents a violation of the rights of all women who believe in the social and moral values of womanhood [5]

This fiasco cost taxpayers five million dollars! I'm sure that a large part of the blame must be placed on those in charge of these conferences. Forty-one of the forty-two member commission were pro-abortion and pro-womens' liberation. Bella Abzug was the chairman. As a former congresswoman, she introduced a "gay rights" bill as an amendment to the Civil Rights Bill. It did not pass. She sponsored the bill authorizing 5 million dollars to fund the state and national IWY conferences. Her first official directive, after she was appointed, advised each state IWY chairman to add a workshop on "sexual preference" (lesbianism). Another member was Gloria Steinam, editor of *Ms.* Steinam said in one speech:

> For those who wish to live in equal partnership, we have to abolish and reform the institution of legal marriage. . . . By the year 2000, we will, I hope, raise our children to believe in human potential, not in God. [6]

Other members included Jean O'Leary, co-executive director of the National Gay Task Force: Eleanor Smeal, who became president of the National Organization for Women (she said she removed her wedding band because it symbolized that she belonged to somebody); Martha Griffiths, the principle ERA sponsor in Congress; and Jill Ruckleshause, who is pro-abortion and pro-ERA.

What does all this have to do with us? If the end result is to be used as a "blueprint" for future legislation, then it does affect us. Laws affect our lives daily, involving our children and grandchildren.

A basic objective of the women's liberationists is to neuterize sexist terms in all laws, textbooks, and language of the news media. Some state legislatures ordered computer printouts of all laws that use such "sexist" words as *man, woman, husband,* and *wife.* They were to be replaced with neuter equivalents.[7] Since our schools hold a "captive audience" of almost every member in our society, some radical feminists and homosexuals are going all out to use them as a tool for social change.

The feminists look upon textbooks as a major weapon in their campaign to eliminate what they call our "sex-stereotyped society" and to restructure it into one that is sex-neutral from cradle to grave. Under liberationist demands, the Macmillan Publishing Company issued a booklet called "Guidelines for Creating Positive Sexual and Racial Images in Educational Materials." Its purpose is to instruct authors in the use of sex-neutral language, concepts, and illustrations to conform to the new Macmillan censorship code. The McGraw-Hill Book Company has issued a similar pamphlet.

For example, you should not say "mankind"; it should be "humanity." You should not say "brotherhood"; it should be "amity." The section for eliminating sexism in textbook illustrations is even more amusing: A father pictured doing household chores and nursing a sick child; a mother working at her desk while dad clears the dining room table; a boy preening in front of a mirror; and a man using hair spray. The guidelines warn that books indicating that "homemaking" is a vocation primarily for women will not be tolerated. In *The Castrated Family*, the author states:

> Men are having effeminate styles forced upon them and many men seem to eagerly accept these styles. Long hair, scented bodies, handbags, earrings, are the adornment of women. When a man is willing to be influenced by these trends he is demonstrating his weakness. Women's styles are increasingly sexless or masculine. Note that not only are pantsuits popular for women, but that the zipper which was once at the side has been shifted to the front where the man's zipper is placed. I have no doubt that the creators of these styles come from disturbed families and are, as a consequence, not fully masculine or feminine. . . . Clothing and hair styles have a feedback effect on the individual and in time will influence his self-concept. . . . The trend is toward a unisex society and we are close to having this trend reinforced by constitutional amendment (ERA). Apparently unaware of the difference between equal opportunity and equal ability, or unable to stand up to pressure groups such as NOW, just as weak men within the family cannot stand up to aggressive wives, the Congress has forced industry and our armed forces to accept women into positions which only men should occupy.[8]

Not only are the schools being used in the instigation of social changes concerning traditional roles of men and women in occupation and dress, but also in the transformation of attitudes concerning sexuality and family life. Adverse propaganda now shown to many of our teenagers in the name of sex education is more dangerous than most people realize.

Two examples provide a clear picture. Although I did not view the following films, the two pamphlets describing them adequately portray the films' contents.

The first film, on the subject of lesbianism, is entitled *Lavender*—"A sensitive, honest approach to an often misunderstood aspect of human sexuality." The descriptive pamphlet includes excerpts from the authentic narration and stills (pictures) from the original footage. Here are two examples:

ON BEING GAY AND RELIGIOUS
I remember you were kind of disappointed when I told you
I dropped out of the seminary. But I think now you understand why I had to tell the school that I am a lesbian. If they
do readmit me, I can get my academic degree, then maybe
in ten years or so the church will come around and I can go
ahead and get ordained.

ON BEING HUMAN
. . . you know, there's something really comforting in wak-
ing up in the morning and feeling a nice, warm human
body lying there, and knowing that you can roll over and
say, "Good morning."

The intent of the film is obvious after reading the
"Suggested Uses and Discussion Topics" section of the
pamphlet.

Lavender is a very useful film in gently yet openly introducing high school students to this delicate area of sexuality. It can also be very helpful in relieving the many mis-
understandings and fears that accompany newfound adolescent emotions. Here are a couple of questions which can
be raised:
1. How can the students better understand and deal
with the natural and yet frightening feelings they have for
their peers?
2. What sort of attitude did they have toward homosex-
uality and lesbianism before?
3. Has this film opened up any new areas of thought?

A note about the producer of the film appears on the
back of the pamphlet.

She strongly believes that the film can be used to re-
educate and responsibly influence social patterns [italics mine]
and subsequently has used her film making . . .

Here it is openly admitted that the point of the film is
to influence others into a homosexual behavior pattern,
or to at least accept this type of relationship.
The other film, entitled Valerie, presents a transvestite (a

male who dresses like a woman) who is a prostitute. The pamphlet refers to him as "her" with the following observations about the film:

> An intensely personal account of a life-style understood by few people: the story of a transvestite.

This conclusion is drawn:

> In all, "Valerie" comes across as a very real person, not so terribly different from the people she shocks and surprisingly sure of her values.

Many would join me in exclaiming, "*What* values?" A further shock comes in the discovery that the U.S. Department of Health, Education, and Welfare recommends the use of these films. *Lavender*, for example, has these suggested uses printed on the front of the pamphlet:

> High School, College, Adult Education, P.T.A. Programs, Women's Organizations, Public Libraries, Health Agencies, Social Workers.

I've heard this statement several times: "If God doesn't judge America, He'll have to apologize to Sodom and Gomorrah on "Judgment Day." I guess the only reason He hasn't is because there are "ten righteous men"—a strong and vocal concerned minority—still fighting for His ways.

Linda Burnett

Psychiatric Comment

Many complaints by women's liberation advocates are legitimate. One of our best friends is a female lab technician who gets a couple hundred dollars a month less than male lab technicians with the same amount of training and experience. That's not right. And I believe that God calls many women to make significant contributions to society through professional careers. I get very angry however, when I hear feminists criticize and downgrade other women for choosing to be housewives or for submitting to their husband's authority. Being a housewife is a calling from God that is just as worthwhile as any other calling, and frequently a lot more difficult.

I thank God frequently for my godly mother. I am also grateful for the elderly, unmarried woman in my home church who prayed for me every day while I was in high school. What an impact she made on my life!

Many people are surprised to find out that the ideal, godly woman described in Proverbs 31 had servant girls help her at home so she could have time to invest in a little real estate (v. 16); do a little farming (v. 16); and make garments to sell commercially (v. 24). But she also "watches over the affairs of her household," and is never lazy (v. 27). Moreover, she is a great help to her husband and richly satisfies his needs (vv. 11–12).

In her book, *Hidden Art,* Edith Schaeffer shows numerous ways in which godly women can be creative in the home, making good use of their God-given talents.[9] She says that much of the impetus for the women's liberation movement comes from frustrated housewives who aren't expressing their creativity in the home. Every Christian woman should read this book.

Although feminists have some legitimate complaints, I am aware of some morally corrupt trends within the movement, such as the call by some to make war against God's Word and God Himself. As a psychiatrist, I resist their denunciation of male authority in the home, since the vast majority of neurotics I encounter come from homes dominated by women. Janet Zollinger Giele, of Radcliffe Institute in Cambridge, Massachusetts, stated that our young people "have been steeped in the new morality, the new psychology, the experience of mechanization and the interchangeability of personnel. It took only a small step to extend these principles to sex roles."[10] She added that "recent demographic trends indicate a shift in the parental and marital roles of both men and women. . . . The nature of the family is being transformed as the worlds of women and men increasingly overlap."[11] This is especially true of women born since the depression of the 1930s. I hope it won't take another great depression to bring us to our senses. Ironically, the attacks by extreme feminists against traditional family life come dangerously close to the assault on the biblically-patterned home by the communist theorist Karl Marx, who taught that "the patriarchal family must go because it is the chief institution that oppresses and enslaves women."[12] Even Dr. Henry Greenbaum, a psychiatrist and Freudian analyst who is pro-women's liberation in general, states that the movement is attacking marriage, family, and parenthood, which are essential human needs. He asserts that these trends will "lower the quality of life."[13] He also astutely observes that "whatever form our evolving institutions do take will depend to a great extent on our moral value systems and the quality of people."[14]

Paul Meier, M.D.

Notes

1. Edward Hunter, *The Black Book of Red China* (1958) as quoted in *The Women's Lib, Equal Rights Amendment* (Long Beach, Calif.: Concerned Americans), p. 5.

2. Barbara Galewski, "Why I Oppose the ERA—I Saw It in Sweden," *The Women's Lib, Equal Rights Amendment* (Concerned Americans), p. 5.

3. Rosemary Thomson, *The Price of Liberty* (Carol Stream, Ill.: Creation House, 1978), p. 31.

4. Report of the Fall 1979 Television Monitoring Program of the National Federation for Decency, Tupelo, Miss.

5. U.S. Congress, Senate, *Congressional Record,* Vol. 123, No. 194 (7 December 1977), p. S19425.

6. Gloria Steinam in a speech given in Houston, *Saturday Review of Education,* March 1973, p. 17.

7. Phyllis Schlafly, *The Power of the Positive Woman* (New Rochelle, NY: Arlington House, 1977). p. 25.

8. Harold Voth, *The Castrated Family* (Mission, Kan.: Sheed Andrews and McMeel, 1977), pp. 208, 220.

9. Edith Schaeffer, *Hidden Art* (Wheaton, IL: Tyndale House, 1971).

10. Janet Zollinger Giele, "Changes in the Modern Family: Their Impact on Sex Roles," *American Journal of Orthopsychiatry* 41 (October 1971): 757–766.

11. Ibid.

12. Quoted in Alice S. Rossi, "Family Development in a Changing World," *American Journal of Psychiatry* 128 (March 1972): 1057–1066.

13. Henry Greenbaum, "Marriage, Family and Parenthood," *American Journal of Psychiatry,* 131 (November 1973): 1262–1265.

14. Ibid.

7

The Fulfilled Mother

At a party, a career woman asked my sister-in-law, "Don't you want to contribute something to society?" Evidently this woman felt that raising children was not a sufficiently worthy contribution to society. Not the least bit apologetic, my sister-in-law replied, "I feel like I'm doing more by bestowing three healthy, well-adjusted, happy people to society than I ever could by choosing a profession."

Regrettably, many women believe that giving one's life to meeting the emotional and physical needs of a man and dependent children is not as important as cleaning teeth, teaching, or even being a doctor. To me, these other careers pale against the awesome calling to help shape the capabilities, the drives, and the dreams of the next generation.

A case in point is Susanna Wesley, who has been called the mother of Methodism. It is easy to trace the influence of her mind and character upon both her distinguished sons, Charles, the song writer, and John, the evangelist. "She deliberately set out to give his (John's) soul the shape which she believed it ought to have."[1]

When John Wesley was six years old, he narrowly escaped burning to death in his father's parsonage at Epworth. That day, Susanna Wesley made the following entry in her diary:

> Son John, what shall I render to the Lord for all his mercies? I would offer myself and all that Thou hast given me; and I would resolve, O, give me grace to do it! that the residue of my life shall be all devoted to Thy service. And I do intend to be more particularly careful with the soul of this child, that Thou has so mercifully provided for, than ever I have been; that I may instill in his mind the principles of true religion and virtue. Lord, give me grace to do it sincerely and prudently.[2]

John Wesley wrote that one reason why he married later in life was because he earlier despaired of ever meeting another woman "like my father's wife." John was the fifteenth of Susanna's nineteen children, nine of whom died at an early age. This talented woman wrote three elementary books on Christian theology for the instruction of her children. She taught them as a class, and once a week she had a private conference with each child.

What was Susanna's view of her role as a mother? Her son Samuel once began a letter to her with "Madame." She wrote back: "Sammy, I do not love distance and ceremony. There is more love and tenderness in the name of mother than in all the complimental titles in the world."[3]

A Woman's Credentials

God created women not only with the special emotional, mental, and physical equipment to meet their husbands' needs, but to meet the unique needs of their children as well. Obviously, the woman is especially made to meet the physical needs of a newborn infant (i.e., milk). Just as women's bodies are uniquely designed, I also believe that God has given women a special emotional makeup (i.e. patience and understanding) for raising children.

God created Adam and Eve in His image. We should reflect Him in our lives because of it. His first directive to His new creations was to "be fruitful and increase in number; fill the earth and subdue it" (Gen. 1:28). Don Meredith, of *Christian Family Life,* suggests three directives from God as a *purpose* for our lives—the three R's: (1) Reflect God's glory; (2) Reign in spiritual warfare; and (3) Reproduce a godly heritage.

Even if some of God's plans for me are obscure at this point in my life, there is one thing I do know: I am to reproduce a godly heritage in this world for His glory.

In realizing my calling as a mother, believing that the Lord has so equipped me, I can move ahead in confidence, knowing that, God "who calls you is faithful and he will do it" (1 Thess. 5:24).

When I first told one of my sisters-in-law about writing this book and what I was going to put in it, she said, "That's all well and fine—but you've forgotten something. You've stated all the reasons why a woman should stay home for her kid's sake. How about hers? Can *she* be fulfilled by being just a mother?" I relayed what happened to me that day to explain why I felt that a woman could be fulfilled in this role, or any role, if she were a Christian.

As I was driving home from the shopping center, I noticed a pathetic-looking person walking by the road. He wore old clothes and had no shoes. If that wasn't pitiful enough, he was limping. "Why," I asked myself "would a God of love allow anyone to be in such a sad state?" And God gave me this insight: Does my happiness depend on the clothes I wear? No—my personal happiness is dependent on whether I'm walking with the Lord. Then it hit me. That man, if he's walking with Jesus could be happier right now than most unsaved people will ever be! He could even be happier than some Christians who have never unlocked the power and peace that Jesus makes available.

Because we were created by and for God, our happiness is dependent upon our fellowship with Him. Saint Augustine expressed that every man is born with a God-shaped vacuum, and his soul is restless until he finds rest in Him.

How do we find God—that is, come into a relationship with Him? It can happen because He wants fellowship with us! He has instigated a relationship with us already. First, we must realize what we are by *God's* standards. "For all have sinned and fall short of the glory of God" (Rom. 3:23). The Bible also tells us: "But God demonstrates his own love for us in this: While we were still sinners, Christ died for us" (Rom. 5:8). *Why* did Christ have to die for us? Paul has the answer: "God presented him [Christ] as a sacrifice of atonement, through faith in his blood. He did this to demonstrate his justice . . . so as to be just and the one who justifies the man who has faith in Jesus" (Rom. 3:25,26).

We are sinners by God's standard (His standard is perfection). Because God is holy He couldn't allow us to live eternally with Him in a sinful state. *Someone* had to pay the penalty for our sins. Therefore, He sent His only Son so that all who believe in Him may not die but have eternal life (cf. John 3:16). Heaven is a free gift from God. "The gift of God is eternal life in Christ Jesus our Lord" (Rom. 6:23).

You don't have to work your way into a right relationship with God—in fact, you can't. You simply agree with God that you are a sinner and trust what Christ already accomplished in paying the penalty for your sins. What Christ accomplished includes coming to earth to be the Messiah, shedding His blood on the cross for our sins, dying, and rising from the grave. Being in His presence is joy unspeakable. And we can fellowship with Him any time we want.

How do we *maintain* this fellowship? By talking and listening to Him (through reading the Bible and praying) and by obeying what He tells us to do. It's important to remember that as believers we don't lose our relationship with Him. We are His children forever. When our own children are unkind or disobedient, there may be a temporary break in their fellowship with us, but our relationship with them is still the same—they are ours regardless. God relates to us in the same way.

Although our *relationship* is not in jeopardy when we disobey God, our happiness is certainly affected. "Now that you know these things, you will be blessed if you do them" (John 13:17). Christ said, "whoever has my commands and obeys them, he is the one who loves me. He who loves me will be loved by my father, and I, too, will love him and show myself to him" (John 14:21). What more could we want in life than to be secure in God's love for us through Jesus Christ?

After the time in my life when I willfully put my son's needs above my own, joy filled my life because I was no longer a slave to self-gratification. Joy will increase as I continue to trust Jesus with every aspect of my life.

One of the most beautiful rewards the Bible assures to a woman who is God's woman is: "Her children arise and call her blessed" (Prov. 31:28).

I'll never forget what happened to me while I was a student at the University of Arkansas. I asked a fellow student, who had missed the previous class, if she had been sick. "Naw, I had to go to a funeral," she said. "I'm sorry," I responded. "Were you very close to the person?" "No," she replied "it was my dad. I didn't even like him."

I could tell that she was sincere. I was numb. I could not comprehend this lack of affection.

She was only one of thousands who never experience a strong love relationship with their parents as God intended. I felt hurt not only for this girl who lacked love for her own father, but also for the man who hadn't been the father he was created to be. He had rarely experienced his child's love and admiration.

Several years ago I enclosed a brief note with a gift to my mother on Mother's Day. The Scripture on it was: "Now we see but a poor reflection; then [in heaven] we shall see face to face. Now I know in part; then I shall know fully" (1 Cor. 13:12). To this verse, I added: "You'll never know how much I love you until you're in heaven." My mother still keeps this note on her bulletin board as a constant reminder of my love for her. She knows the joy of the words, "Her children arise and call her blessed." I cannot now express all my love for her as well as for my father since their love for me over the years *has* been expressed in countless acts of love and commitment.

The apostle Paul stated "If I have the gift of prophesy and can fathom all mysteries and all knowledge, and if I have a faith that can remove mountains, but have not love, I am nothing" (1 Cor. 13:2). My prayer for those of you who are young mothers is that you *will* pursue love, because I know that if you do your children will someday rise up and call you blessed.

Linda Burnett

CHILDREN WON'T WAIT[4]

There is a time to anticipate the baby's coming, a time to
    consult a doctor;
A time to plan a diet and exercise, a time to gather a
    Layette.
There is a time to wonder at the ways of God, knowing this
    is the destiny for which I was crafted;
A time to dream of what this child may become,
A time to pray that God will teach me how to train this
    child which I bear.
A time to prepare myself that I might nurture his soul.
But soon there comes the time for birth,
For babies won't wait.

There is a time for night feedings, and colic and formulas.
There is a time for rocking and a time for walking the floor,
A time for patience and self-sacrifice,
A time to show him that his new world is a world of love
    and goodness and dependability.
There is a time to ponder what he is—not a pet nor toy, but
    a person, an individual—a soul made in God's image.
There is a time to consider my stewardship. I cannot
    possess him.
He is not mine. I have been chosen to care for him, to love
    him, to enjoy him, to nurture him, and to answer to
    God.
I resolve to do my best for him,
For babies don't wait.

There is a time to hold him close and tell him the sweetest
   story ever told;
A time to show him God in earth and sky and flower,
   to teach him to wonder and reverence.
There is a time to leave the dishes, to swing him in the
   park.
To run a race, to draw a picture, to catch a butterfly,
   to give him happy comradeship.
There is a time to point the way, to teach his infant lips to
   pray,
To teach his heart to love God's Word, to love God's day.
For children don't wait.

There is a time to sing instead of grumble, to smile instead
   of frown,
To kiss away the tears and laugh at broken dishes.
A time to share with him my best in attitudes—a love of
   life, a love of God, a love of family.
There is a time to answer his questions, all his questions,
Because there may come a time when he will not want my
   answers.
There is a time to teach him so patiently to obey, to put his
   toys away.
There is a time to teach him the beauty of duty, the habit of
   Bible study, the joy of worship at home,
For children don't wait.

There is a time to watch him bravely go to school, to miss
   him underfoot,
And to know that other minds have his attention, but that I
   will be there to answer his call when he comes home,
And listen eagerly to the story of his day.
There is a time to teach him independence, responsibility,
   self-reliance,
To be firm but friendly, to discipline with love,
For soon, so soon, there will be a time to let go, the apron
   strings untied,
For children won't wait.

There is a time to treasure every fleeting minute of his
   childhood.
Just eighteen precious years to inspire and train him.
I will not exchange this birthright for a mess of pottage
   called social position, or business or professional
   reputation, or a pay check.
An hour of concern today may save years of heartache
   tomorrow,

The house will wait, the dishes will wait, the new room can
    wait,
But children don't wait.

There will be a time when there will be no slamming of
    doors, no toys on the stairs, no childhood quarrels, no
    fingerprints on the wallpaper.
Then may I look back with joy and not regret.
There will be a time to concentrate on service outside my
    home;
On visiting the sick, the bereaved, the discouraged, the
    untaught;
To give myself to the "least of these."
There will be a time to look back and know that these years
    of motherhood were not wasted.
I pray there will be a time to see him an upright and honest
    man, loving God and serving all.
God, give me wisdom to see that today is my day with my
    children.
That there is no unimportant moment in their lives.
May I know that no other career is so precious,
No other work so rewarding,
No other task so urgent.
May I not defer it nor neglect it,
But by thy Spirit accept it gladly, joyously, and by thy
    grace realize
That the time is short and my time is now,
For children won't wait!

Helen M. Young

Psychiatric Comment

These human needs are basic: (1) Self-worth; (2) Intimacy with others; and (3) Intimacy with God. To be *fulfilled* a woman does not have to have children or even be
married. But she does have to fill her God-vacuum with an
intimate relationship with God through faith in Jesus
Christ. Intimacy with God is enhanced by strong bonds of
love with a mate and children. The most satisfied, fulfilled
women I know are those who have intimacy with a hus-

band and children as well as with God. Intimacy with
others and with God brings self-worth.

Paul Meier, M.D.

Notes

1. Abram Lipsky, *John Wesley, A Portrait* (New York: AMS Press, 1927
reproduction), p. 18.
2. Ibid., pp. 18, 19.
3. Ibid., p. 27.
4. Beverly LaHaye, *How To Develop Your Child's Temperament,* (Irvine,
Calif.:, Harvest House Publishers, 1977), pp. 5–8, used by permission.

8

Fallacies of the
Working Mother

Eliza Paschall, then National Secretary for the National Organization for Women, heard one young lady tell another after an N.O.W. seminar: "Those poor housewives don't even *know* how unhappy they are!"

This is typical of many women who have set out to let housewives know just how "bad off" they really are. A housewife today would have to be deaf and blind not to have heard the propaganda that being at home is not only limiting, boring, lonely, and distasteful, but *meaningless* as well. Women are urged to become career persons if they want to contribute significantly to society. To get this message across, however, some myths have been created to make the exodus plausible, even preferable, to the instinctive priority we ascribe to being wives and mothers. Among several myths that have emerged to "enlighten" the "enslaved" female sex, these five are heard most frequently.

Myth One: You Can Have it All

Dr. James Dobson, responding to the issue of preschooler's mothers working, cited this as the number one myth. In writing on what he considered "two equally foolish myths," he stated,

> The first is that *most* mothers of small children can work all day and still come home and meet their family obligations, perhaps even better than they could if they remained at home. Nonsense! There is only so much energy within the human body for expenditure during each twenty-four hours, and when it is invested in one place it is not available for use in another. It is highly improbable that the *average* woman can arise early in the morning and get her family fed and located for the day, then work from 9:00 to 5:00, drive home from 5:01 to 5:30 and still have the energy to assault her "home-work" from 5:31 until midnight. Oh, she may cook dinner and handle the major household chores, but few women alive are equipped with the super strength necessary at the end of a workday to meet the emotional needs of their children, to train and guide and discipline, to build self esteem, to teach the true values of life, and beyond all that, to maintain a healthy marital relationship as well. . . . To the contrary, I have observed that exhausted wives and mothers become irritable, grouchy, and frustrated, setting the stage for conflict within the home.[1]

Even *Ms*, the magazine of the women's movement, included an article that observed:

> . . . many feminists became feminists precisely *because* we have been trying to have it all. We discovered it is simply impossible. Without equal parenting and more societal responsibility and increased flexibility in the work place and at home, there is virtually no person who can do it. *There must* be a systematic political change.[2]

These statements imply that the only answer is role changing—a changing of job descriptions between men and women. If women are to become more like men in their roles (more career oriented), then men will have to take on more of the parenting responsibilities, along with "society."

The *Declaration of Feminism,* states that,

> with the destruction of the nuclear family must come a new
> way of looking at children. They must be seen as the re-
> sponsibility of an *entire society* rather than individual par-
> ents.[3]

Although this philosophy is widespread, it still sur-
prises me to find out that 350,000 children, ages three to
six, are currently being cared for at home by their fathers,
or "house husbands," according to recent Census Bureau
figures.[4]

Myth Two: It Pays to Work

I cannot see working to make money just so that I can
pay someone else to watch my children. Most women
would claim they're not working just for that, but for the
extra things an added income can bring in. But the question is—after the costs of transportation, lunch, new
clothes for work, and child care are deducted—how much
money will be left?

> The cost of preschooler's day-care services added to
> work expenses can easily absorb the total earning of some
> women working full time... Disregarding the costs of
> transportation and other work-connected expenses or the
> imputed cost of performing household tasks in addition to
> work (overtime duty), it is apparent that the daily salary of
> at least half of working women did not provide the cost of a
> single child's day care meeting federal standards.[5]

An issue of *US News & World Report* included:

> Many mothers are finding that after paying for the care
> of their children while they work, there's little profit in
> holding a job.[6]

Colien Hefferan, assistant professor of behavioral economics at Penn State University, states,

> I think many women re-enter the work force without
> any real understanding of the economic consequences. A
> wife may decide she needs to take a job because her hus-
> band is unemployed or is in ill health and the extra in-
> come is essential. Such a woman may feel she's going to
> greatly increase the family's economic well-being; often
> she's wrong. It's important that she weigh all the aspects of
> her decision before she changes her whole life-style for
> something that isn't going to generate all that much
> spendable income.
>
> One thing to keep in mind is that income taxes skim off
> much of the added earnings that result when a wife takes a
> job. The extra pay pushes the family into a higher income
> bracket, and the tax collector gets a bigger portion of their
> total income.
>
> Women don't anticipate what appears at first to be small
> expenses, such as transportation, lunches, social security,
> wear and tear on clothing and automobiles. If one's income
> is relatively low, such expenses can account for 30 or 40
> percent of take-home pay. And if you add child care ... it
> can quickly become more than 50 percent.... A typical
> working wife actually nets in a range of 10 to 30 percent, on
> the average.[7]

My next question touches on one's philosophy of life:
How much does money mean to you? The Bible does not
say "money is the root of all evil," but "the *love* of
money...." Is this money you could be earning necessary
for survival (food or lodging), or is it for added luxuries?
What are those luxuries? Are they more important than
your children? What woman reading this would put her
weekly "beauty parlor" hairdo above her little girl's welfare or even a new car above her little boy's emotional
stability. Yet that is exactly what I'm emphasizing—
priorities. Remember Janet (see chapter one)? She said,
"We love the new house.... We think it's worth it."
Worth what? Perhaps the emotional welfare of her two
girls? I know Janet, and I'm quite sure that if she was

aware of the consequences of her part-time deprivation of
her children, she would *not* think it was "worth it."

Too much importance is placed on money in our society.
Many people measure their *self-worth* with how much
they earn. Perhaps that's one problem with raising children in a capitalist society—parents don't get paid for it.

> One reason work is thought of as so universally worthy is
> that it is universally paid, and people in America too often
> tie the value of what they do to how much money they get
> for doing it.[8]

As for me, my self-worth is grounded in God's love for
me and His intimate concern for my life. If God is "familiar
with all my ways" (Ps. 139:3), what greater value could I
strive for? Whom do I want to impress?

Myth Three: My Children Are Just as Well Off

Dr. Dobson says:

> If this falsehood were accurate, it would conveniently
> expunge all guilt from the consciences of working women.
> But it simply won't square with scientific knowledge. I
> attended a national conference on child development held
> recently in Miami, Florida. Virtually every report of re-
> search presented during that three-day meeting ended
> with the same conclusion: the mother-child relationship is
> absolutely vital to healthy development of children. The
> final speaker of the conference, a well-known authority in
> his field, explained that the Russian government is cur-
> rently abandoning its child-care network because they
> have observed the same inescapable fact: employees of the
> State simply cannot replace the one-to-one influence of a
> mother with her own child.[9]

We know this instinctively. Consequently, most women
who work regardless of whether they need to or not, express guilt because of it.

At one luncheon where I shared some of my research

findings, a woman with a job said, "Don't lay any more guilt on me than I already have—I can't take it." Another woman who had worked for nine months when her son was two, expressed how she still felt deeply guilty about it. She confided, "I went to work to *get away from Matt*. I did not need to work for financial reasons; I just had to get out!" I respect her boldness and honesty. But I ached for her because she admitted that some emotional problems in her son may be related to her working outside the home.

Such guilt is widespread because women instinctively sense how intensely they are needed and, because of it, feel that in some way they have betrayed a trust. The reason people usually *feel* guilty is because they *are* guilty.

Myth Four: Work Is Glamorous and Is My Only Hope for Fulfillment

Jean Dresden Grambs, in an article representative of the women's movement, stated:

> To my mind, working is simply more enjoyable than staying at home... Many women have discovered that working makes you feel free. The control that husbands and fathers have exercised over women rests not merely on tradition, but mainly on the power that derives from being their source of financial support. As such, to the extent it still exists, it is one of the few remaining tyrannies of our social order... women have been damaged by their economic dependence on men. Women... are increasingly exercising their option for the psychological freedom which earning an income provides. *We are on the verge of seeing the establishment of marriages in which neither partner dominates the other or has a prearranged fixed domain of responsibility or authority.* [10]

This statement defies God's principles as much as any I have found, even from the most militant of sources. She asserts that the main reason to work is to get out from under the authority of a husband. But God's Word indeed outlines predetermined roles and responsibilities for men and women, especially pertaining to authority (see Eph. 5:22,23; Col. 3:18; and 1 Peter 3:1).

Our happiness ("fulfillment") is found in finding God's will for our lives, and then living accordingly. We must believe either what we hear in the "world" or what God says in His Word. "But as for me and my household, we will serve the Lord" (Josh. 24:15).

What prompts an average housewife to believe that working outside the home will guarantee fulfillment? Primarily, she finds herself in the middle of a struggle. Life is a struggle, and frequently most all of us find ourselves in undesirable circumstances. A woman in this struggle may be prompted to blame either her mate or her situation. "If I just wasn't stuck at home with the kids all day . . . if I had a job outside the home," she tells herself. (The blame ploy was familiar in the garden,—Adam blamed Eve, and Eve blamed the serpent.) Or, she may rationalize, "If only my husband was the man he should be, then I'd be happy." At this point her commitment is broken. She cannot be committed to something that's not good for her. As her commitment erodes, she rebels, either consciously or subconsciously. Consequently, her dependence on God is severed as well.

Feminists and I disagree on the cause and, therefore, the solution to the housewife's problems. They blame the situation and say that a change of situation (locality) will bring happiness. I believe my happiness comes from within, and my hope is found in realizing and executing what God created me to do.

God, through His Word, has promised me much more than the leaders of the women's movement could ever hope to. A godly perspective of the housewife is presented in Proverbs 31:3–31. "Charm is deceptive, and beauty is fleeting; but a woman who fears the Lord is to be praised. Give her the reward she has earned, and let her works bring her praise at the city gate." Her reward includes her home, her husband, and her children. "The city gate" is a public place. *She will be known by what her home turns out to be!*

A woman in my city is well known in the Christian community. She is "praised in the gates" because *all* five of her children are not only born-again believers but are also mature Christians who follow the Lord's will. Each of them is blessed with a godly mate. This was not a coincidence. God tells us that if we train up our children in the way that they should go, *they will not depart from it!*

Not only will we have the blessing of being praised publicly, but like the woman in Proverbs we will be praised by our husbands as well. Who will notice more how your children turn out than their father?

In addition, like the woman in Proverbs, our children will call us blessed. Don Meredith, founder of *Christian Family Life,* asks,

> Does the woman who succeeds in business or public life get these promises? Like men, the better she does in business, the more competition and jealousy she will experience from men and women alike.[11]

Heart attacks and ulcers are on the increase among women. *Family Weekly* asked Taylor Caldwell, one of the most successful writers of the twentieth century, whether she felt solid satisfaction in knowing that her novel, *Captains and the Kings,* was to be seen as a nine-hour television production. She replied:

> There is no solid satisfaction in any career for a woman like myself. There is no home, no true freedom, no hope, no joy, no expectation for tomorrow, no contentment. I would rather cook a meal for a man and bring him his slippers and feel myself in the protection of his arms than have all the citations and awards and honors I have received worldwide, including the Ribbon of the Legion of Honor and my property and my bank accounts.[12]

Does this successful woman seem "fulfilled?"

Former Israeli premier Golda Meir is widely considered

the outstanding career woman of our time. She achieved more in a man's world than any woman in any country. The Gallop Poll identified her as "the most admired woman" in the world. But she said without hesitation that "having a baby is the most fulfilling thing a woman can ever do."[13]

Should all women get married, have children, and stay at home? Not at all! I believe that some women weren't "cut out" to be mothers. These women would be happier as career women, but they should first decide not to have children.

When Dr. James Dobson was asked this question, he replied,

> A woman should feel free to choose the direction her life will take. In no sense should she be urged to raise a family and abandon her own career or educational objectives, if this is not her desire. . . . My strong criticism, then, is not with those who choose a nonfamily life style for themselves. Rather, it is aimed at those who abandon their parental responsibility after the choice has been made.[14]

Harold M. Voth, a senior psychiatrist and psychoanalyst at the Menninger Foundation, in describing young women who have a hard time establishing a healthy heterosexual relationship, wrote

> It would be much better if such women had never had children in the first place. . . . Those who cannot or choose not to have children deserve society's deepest respect for the sacrifice they make.[15]

I deeply respect Katherine Hepburn for speaking out about herself. She shared:

> People say to me, "Too bad you didn't have any children." Well, I'm not dumb enough to think I could have handled that situation because I'm a totally concentrated person. I can do one thing at a time. I'm a One-Track-Charlie.

If I had a kid, and the kid was desperately ill, and I had an opening night—what am I gonna do? I would be useless. If your mind is on something else, and you are involved in an emotional relationship—you are useless. If someone needs you, they need YOU!

That's why I think women have to choose. I remember making the decision, "Well, I'll never marry and have children. I want to be a star, and I don't want to make my husband my victim. And I certainly don't want to make my children my victims.[16]

Myth Five: Working Is My Contribution to Society

For three reasons this statement is far from the truth. First, unemployment in our society is at an all time high and is one of the most critical problems confronting our nation. If women who work outside of the home for fulfillment rather than financial need would remain home instead, many people who *really need* to work, such as single women with children or other heads of households, could fill job openings.

Second, and more important, American families, which are endangered these days, would be strengthened by following the traditional pattern in which just the husband is the provider. This allows the husband and wife to fulfill distinctive functions for meeting individual needs within the family unit. For example, a woman dependent on her husband financially will likely develop a stronger love, affection, and respect toward him as well. The husband will usually reciprocate with a deeper and more tender love toward his wife as he feels responsible (and proud) in establishing financial security for his family. Wives at home are available to meet the physical needs of their children, which may on the surface seem trivial or routine but actually become experiences that spark the spontaneous love children feel for their mothers. How many mothers recall a surging of tenderness and love while placing a band-aid over a child's stinging knee abrasion as young, misty eyes search a mother's face for reassurance and young ears absorb her soft, comforting words. Family members dependent on each other for physical needs will find their emotional needs better fulfilled and their mutual love thriving.

By contrast, if both the husband and wife are financially independent (of each other) because both work outside the home, the feeling of interdependence between them diminishes and the bond of intimacy erodes too easily. For both children and parents, economic and physical dependency within the family unit generates emotional stability. Columbia University sociologist Amitia Etzioni says, "The family has already lost its economic function as women become more financially independent."[17] He stresses further that the institutionalization of day care would endanger the family's other key reason for being—raising children.

> If we take the ultimate function of the family and bureaucratize it, then we might as well close up shop.[18]

And, finally, what better contribution can any parent make to society than to bestow to it emotionally stable and wholesome young people who will be productive and happy adults and become the leaders for tomorrow's challenges and crises.

Linda Burnett

Psychiatric Comment

Nearly all of us feel inferior from time to time. People are naturally inclined to compensate for inferiority feelings in three ways (cf. 1 John 2:15–16 KJV):

1. Lust of the Flesh

Lusting of the flesh includes such sins as pursuing extramarital affairs, viewing pornography, and excessively indulging in sexual fantasies. By actually having or imagining someone other than our mate as a sexual partner gives a temporary, false feeling of significance. After counseling hundreds of people involved in illicit affairs, I am convinced that if everyone was free of inferiority feelings and possessed genuine self-worth, there would be hardly any such affairs.

One "hidden agenda" motivating many young mothers to work full-time is conscious or unconscious desire to get male attention. This is especially true of females with hysterical tendencies, who grew up being either ignored by their fathers or else smothered by their fathers as a "pet." Those deprived of fatherly attention in childhood compensate with an enormous craving for the attention of "father-figures" (other male authority figures of any age). Those who were spoiled by their fathers as father's "pet" (many of whom were even sexually approached by their fathers) have a craving to continue the "pet" tradition by being the "pet" of other male authority figures. Thus, the appeal to go to work may involve conscious or unconscious sexual motives, even in Christian women.

2. Lust of the Eyes

Basically, this includes the desire to spend extravagantly —far beyond meeting our necessities (materialism). Who can deny that buying nice things (clothes, jewelry, cars, and household items) gives a temporary feeling of significance. But it never lasts. John D. Rockefeller was once asked by a reporter, "How much money will it take to make you happy?" Rockefeller looked her straight in the eye and said, "Just a little bit more." Materialism is one of the primary psychological forces pulling mothers into full-time employment and leaving their young children in day-care centers. This occurs because they feel inferior, and our current cultural trends reinforce inferiority feelings among housewives. Thus, women enter the job market to earn money to buy things that they are misguided into believing will make them feel significant.

3. The Pride of Life

This fundamentally includes the drive for social status and power. Before World War II, a housewife who abandoned her children to daily child-care so she could enter the job market was viewed as a selfish woman and a prospect for divorce. Today, divorce or no divorce, doing this same thing is a status symbol. Moreover, dedicated mothers and housewives are looked down upon as psychologically-abused masochists.

Getting a job and doing well at it *can* help a person's self-worth. I have encouraged many housewives who were either childless or had grown children to seek employment for the sake of their feelings of self-worth. Some mothers of school-age children can find part-time employment very satisfying through a work schedule that makes room for responsible mothering. But I do not recommend that mothers of preschoolers work full time. Neither would I recommend that mothers of school-age children (under eighteen) work full time. It would be too demanding for most women. Unfortunately, some mothers are forced to work because of divorce or the death of the mate. Whatever the conditions, however, the guilt that will eventually come to women who neglect their own children's needs so they can work will negate any potential temporary feeling of self-worth their jobs may bring.

The most enduring way for anyone to drive for significance is a genuine relationship with Jesus Christ and with at least one other human being. The ideal situation for a significant life is intimacy with God, mate, children, eventually grandchildren, and two or three friends of the same sex. Again, man's three basic needs are (1) Self-worth; (2) Intimacy with others, and (3) Intimacy with God. A wise person will meet these basic needs in God's ways. The three ways of the world—the lust of the flesh, the lust of the eyes, and the pride of life (cf. 1 John 2:15–16)—will not satisfy, except for the moment.

Paul Meier, M.D.

Notes

1. James Dobson, *What Wives Wish Their Husbands Knew About Women* (Wheaton, IL: Tyndale House, 1975), p. 56.
2. Letty Cottin Poegrebin, "Can Women Really Have It All?—Should We?" *Ms*, March 1978, pp. 47–48.
3. Nancy Lehmann and Helen Sullinger, "The Document: Declaration of Feminism" (Minneapolis).
4. Census Bureau figures 1978, cited by Charlette Saikowski, *Christian Science Monitor* News Service.
5. Sara Levitan and Karen Cleary Alderman, *Child Care and ABCs Too* (Baltimore: Johns Hopkins University Press, 1976), p. 44.
6. *U.S. News & World Report*, 12 April 1976, pp. 49–50.
7. Colien Hefferan, *U.S. News & World Report*, 4 December 1976, pp. 49–50.
8. Marjorie Boyd, "The Case Against Day Care," *The Washington Monthly*, 1976, p. 31.
9. Dobson, *What Wives Wish Their Husbands Knew*, p. 56.
10. Jean Dresden Grambs, ed., "Working Mothers—the Wonder Women," *Parents Magazine*, April 1977, p. 33.
11. Seminar sponsored by *Christian Family Life*.
12. Quoted in Phyllis Schlafly, *The Power of the Positive Woman* (New Rochelle, NY: Arlington House, 1977), p. 48.
13. Ibid., p. 47.
14. Dobson, *What Wives Wish Their Husbands Knew*, p. 58.
15. Harold Voth, *The Castrated Family* (Mission, KS: Sheed Andrews and McMeel, 1977), p. 200.
16. Quoted in Schafly, *The Power of the Positive Woman*, p. 42.
17. *U.S. News & World Report*, 15 January 1979.
18. Ibid.

9

For Those Without a Choice

Some women have no choice but to work—because of divorce or death, or a very low income. If you are one of these, please understand that this book was not written for you, but for those women who have entered the work force for reasons other than real need (because of peer pressure, media push for fulfillment outside of motherhood, or selfishness—combined with the false assumption that their children are as well off, or better off, in a day-care situation).

I feel deeply sympathetic about your circumstances. Although this book is written about what is ideal for children, I will share with you, based on my findings, what is the *second* best alternative for your child.

Second Best Substitute

All of us must face the main problem with day care: that the care of the children is mainly impersonal custodial care because many women work with many different children. Therefore, the best substitute for your child in your absence would be *one* woman who keeps children in her home. This is usually called a home-based day-care facility. With this choice, you can be assured that your child will have the opportunity to develop an intimate relationship with another adult, and hopefully that mother-figure will learn your child's special, individual needs (when he cries—is he hungry? hurting? scared? anxious?). Therefore, in a home-based day-care facility, your child's needs are more likely to be met.

Also, family day-care usually costs less than group care, and it provides other advantages for parent and child, such as convenience, flexibility and familiarity.[1]

First of all, contact your local social service agent to see which home-based facilities are licensed and which ones have openings. In my state, according to Jean Martin, Executive Director, Arkansas Family Daycare Providers for Quality Childcare, only one out of ten are licensed. I was also informed that the licensing is not strict at all. Most states share a similar problem.

Also, you could ask working mothers you know where their children are cared for. And lastly, a notice at church might prove fruitful.

When investigating a home-based day-care facility, be concerned not only with the physical surroundings (play area, cleanliness) but also remember that the caregiver herself is the key to the quality of your child's experience in home-based day care.

Some Problems to Watch For

In any day-care situation you select, some problems are inevitable. A home-based day-care situation is no exception.

I can think of two. First, you must allow, and even *encourage*, your child to develop a deep love-relationship with another woman. This is extremely difficult for most mothers. At a Bible study I attended, for example, I overheard a little two-year-old call her mother "Suzy." "Oh, that's the name of the woman who keeps her for me," she said when she noticed how surprised I looked. She continued, "Sometimes she gets us mixed up." I could tell it didn't bother her much. But I would guess that she's an exception. When the National Council of Jewish Women studied day care and all it entailed, they interviewed many mothers, whose comments were published in the book, *Windows on Day Care*. A typical statement was, "I don't like it when the baby calls grandma 'mother'."[2] From these interviews the author of the book concluded, "Some mothers talked of their concern that in a home situation a small child may identify too closely with the substitute mother and resentment easily builds up."[3]

The second problem that could occur is what to do if the one day-care substitute you have becomes ill or cannot watch your child for some personal reason on a particular day. You may have to prepare youself to take a day off from work or make a prior arrangement with a friend to take your child for such a day.

Lastly, no matter how well you might screen a prospective day-care situation, it is impossible to know for sure that your child will experience positive stimuli. A woman in San Jose, California, told an interviewer for the National Council of Jewish Women, "My two little boys have never known the security of a regular family life, with a mother at home. There has been a constant shifting of day-care homes—some very good, a few resulting in nearly traumatic experiences. The insecurity has resulted in many emotional problems in my older boy."[4]

A good guarantee for protecting your child against most bad experiences is to be sure that the prospective caretaker is a spirit-filled Christian. You then can be assured that she will love him with the love of Christ. God knows your situation, and if He has allowed it to come into your life, He will be faithful to meet that particular need. You can rest on the Bible's promise that, "He who did not spare his own Son, but gave him up for us all, how will he not also, along with him, graciously give us all things?" (Rom. 8:32).

Linda Burnett

Psychiatric Comment

As a psychiatrist, I have attempted to help scores of women who, as mothers of young children, have been widowed or victimized by unwanted divorce. Many have wept in my office, deeply concerned for their children while searching for the best solution among unwelcomed alternatives. The following series of questions and replies typify the questions most frequently asked by these mothers and the advice that my associates or myself generally share with them.

Question: I am the only parent for my two preschool children. I have to work, although I don't want to. Where can I leave my children while I work—and feel assured that they will receive good care?

Reply: Are there other sources of income you could live on, which would allow you to remain home with your children until they are in school all day? If not, what is the least amount of money you and your children could get by on until they are in school all day? In the long run, your children are much better off having you at home with them than having a better standard of living now.

Is there a money-making job you could do in your own home (sewing or tailoring clothes for a clothing store, typing research papers for college students, or some other creative alternatives)? Some of my former students have built thriving businesses of their own out of ideas they thought of when forced to earn incomes at their homes.[5]

If you must work outside your home, can you find a job nearby to save travel time and expense? Will your boss allow you to come home during the lunch hour? Would your boss agree to let you work two-thirds of a normal workday so you can get home earlier? Do you have a trustworthy relative or friend nearby who would lovingly care for your children while you work? At least your child would be in a loving home atmosphere rather than in the more impartial environment of a day-care center.

Question: I am a single parent, and I have no responsible relatives or friends nearby who would care for my two preschool children while I work outside of the home. I have tried to find some work or business to do in my home, but because I live in a small town I haven't found anything that will adequately support my children and me. I have no outside sources of income to help me through the years while my children are of preschool age.

But I have found a forty hour-a-week job near our apartment that pays fairly well and is not too much of a drain on me. I must place my preschoolers in a day-care center because it is the only type of care available.

Reply: Have you asked your pastor whether he knows of any Christians who you could pay to watch your children lovingly? Have you called other pastors in your area? Have you looked for a home based day-care facility? Is there a church based, Christian day-care center in your community? Day-long care for your children at a church based center may still be psychologically damaging to your children, but a Christian staff likely will be more loving, more genuinely concerned with the welfare of your children, and less interested in how much financial profit they can get through caring for your children. When a day-care facility becomes the only possible choice, I recommend searching for one with the following child-staff ratio:

AGE OF THE CHILD	NUMBER OF CHILDREN FOR ONE STAFF MEMBER*
One	One-to-One
Two	Two-to-One
Three	Three-to-One
Four	Four-to-One
Five	Five-to-One

*Direct, personal care

Question: I am the mother of three preschool children, and I find myself becoming increasingly bored from staying at home with them all day, every day. But I really don't want to leave my children with other care-takers if it would be psychologically damaging to them. My husband earns an adequate living for necessities, but it would be nice to have a little spending money of my own to buy a few extras for myself and my children. I also feel that I need a change-of-pace activity that would get me away from the children occasionally—for the sake of my sanity. What do you recommend?

Reply: I am convinced that a mother will *benefit* psychologically through taking some "breaks" away from her children. You will likely be a better and more patient mother during the times you spend with your children if you find some times to be away from them doing something you really enjoy.

Your children also will be better off through spending a little time away from you. They will be less dependent on you and will develop more adequate self-concepts by seeing themselves as separate individuals rather than as extensions of you. Full-time day-care, however, has been proven to be psychologically damaging to children. Based on my research and personal experiences with friends and patients, I recommend the following quantities of time for each child to spend away from his parents (and for parents to be away from the child):

AGE OF THE CHILD	NUMBER OF FOUR-HOUR, DAYTIME PERIODS EACH WEEK THAT A CHILD SHOULD (IDEALLY) SPEND AWAY FROM BOTH PARENTS—BUT WITH A LOVING CARE-TAKER OR ADEQUATELY STAFFED NURSERY SCHOOL
One	One
Two	Two
Three	Three
Four	Four
Five	Five

In addition to times away from your children during the day, you and your husband should also go out on a date (by yourselves or with other couples) one or two evenings a week. This is especially beneficial if you can arrange to leave before the children's bedtime hour.

Now let's take a look at some of the options for what you can do with those four-hour periods away from your children. Do you have a job lined up that would really be fulfilling and fun and not too stressful? Does your husband approve of your working part-time? Why does he feel the way he does about it? Would you find more fulfillment if you spent those half-days involved in a Bible study? Would you prefer volunteer work at a hospital? Have you considered taking interesting courses to further your education? Does a hobby interest you for those half-days, such as tennis, needlepoint, golf, or country painting? Your final choice may be an interesting part-time job, and there's nothing wrong with that. But before you start a part-time job, I suggest that you spend one week thinking about it, praying about it, and discussing all of your options with friends who have tried some of them. Then discuss your options with your husband, and be sure that you both agree on the choice you make.

Question: I am the mother of two preschool children and the victim of an unwanted divorce. I admit that our marital conflicts were partially my fault, but I did everything I could to save our marriage. Before the divorce was finalized, I got involved in weekly counseling.

But my husband left me for another woman and divorced me against my wishes. Now I find myself isolated within my church. I am no longer allowed to teach Sunday school because of my church's policy about divorcees. I feel uncomfortable in the couples' class, of which I have been a member for years. Since I am alone, even my married friends feel awkward about having me over for dinner, because of their husbands. Some liberal churches would accept me readily, but I prefer to keep attending a Bible-believing fellowship. But no one in my church has offered to help me with my children, and I'm especially angry about that! Aren't my children the church's responsibility too?

Reply: Since your husband has deserted you and your children and refuses to help you care for them, meeting their physical, emotional, and spiritual needs is primarily your responsibility. But your church also has some God-given responsibility to help with the pressing needs of both you and your children. The Bible, in various passages, is clear on this point. For example, in James 1:27, the Bible says:

> Religion that God our Father accepts as pure and faultless is this: to look after orphans and widows in their distress and to keep oneself from being polluted by the world.

A woman victimized by an unwanted divorce can easily experience much more stress and grief than a woman who loses her partner through death. Children, as well, have much more difficulty coping with their daddy's leaving voluntarily than if their daddy had died. As a divorcee you are a "widow" indeed, and your children are more than fatherless—they are abandoned by him. Because God loves people, He hates divorce and its devastating effects on people. I am sure that God wants your church to provide your children with some healthy father-figures with whom they can identify. I also believe that it is God's will for your church to help *you* in various ways as well.

I understand why you feel angry at your church, but holding a grudge against them would be sinful on your part. How can you handle your anger constructively and find a way to forgive? There are some positive options. Have you considered sharing these pent-up feelings with your pastor, friends, and the Sunday school couples' class? Could you do this in a constructive rather than vengeful manner? Should they continue to neglect you after you confronted them tactfully, what other alternatives are open to you? Are there other evangelical churches that are more accepting of persons in your position although they hate divorce itself?

Paul Meier, M.D.

Notes

1. Dorothy Rodriguez and William F. Hignett, "Guidelines for the Selection of Home-Based Caregivers," *Child Welfare* 55, no. 1 (January 1976): 20–26.

2. Mary Dublin Kerserling, "A Report Based on Findings of the National Council of Jewish Women," *Windows on Day-Care* (New York: National Council of Jewish Women), p. 184.

3. Ibid., p. 183.

4. Ibid., p. 182.

5. Edith Flowers Kilgo, *Money in the Cookie Jar: The Christian Homemaker's Guide to Making Money at Home* (Grand Rapids: Baker Book House Company, 1980). This is solid, sane advice, from a Christian perspective, showing how any average homemaker can find time for a home business without sacrificing church time, family time, or other civic service opportunities. The author includes practical advice on licenses, taxes, bookkeeping, social security, wholesale buying, and advertising.

10

The Aborted Generation

Most people are unaware that the death camps in Germany were not originally set up for the Jews. They were established for the unwanted life of Germany: the unproductive, the deformed, and the crippled—all human life that was an embarrassment to the "master race" and the Third Reich. They were killed by the thousands. An elderly German nun, who had worked with mentally retarded children, reported:

> Our babies were killed. The soldiers came in here, and they took them out, and they threw them like sacks of garbage into their vans, and they took them away, and they killed them because they were retarded.[1]

Ironically, since Hitler lacked sanity himself, one of the first groups he wanted eliminated were the mentally insane. This madness extended to ordering disabled veterans from the first war killed because they were "unproductive."

Amazingly, some of Germany's doctors, who had previously sworn to protect and enrich human lives, became Hitler's executioners. Part of the oath doctors take states: "... I will maintain the utmost respect for human life from the time of conception; even under threat. I will not use my medical knowledge contrary to the laws of humanity. . . ." What distorted the philosophy of these doctors, and the philosophy of other German citizens? What caused them to substitute pragmatism for morality? It did not happen suddenly. It developed and spread subtly. One factor was the growing acceptance of abortion as a means of birth control. This gradually promoted the belief that the end does justify the means. Few can forget Albert Schweitzer's words, "If a man loses reverence for any part of life, he will lose his reverence for all of life."

What is the recent opinion on abortion in West Germany? Delegates of the German Medical Association voted 98 percent against abortion-on-demand. When Jack and Barbara Willke asked them why, they were told "because we've been through this once before and we know what it will lead to."[2]

Eventually, Hitler's purge got around to the aged. After all, what was *useful* was of value, and the aged had passed their days of usefulness. What good were they to the master race?

Their propaganda included showing films to young children in school. One film showed a doctor entering a room of a nursing home and injecting a lethal solution into the arm of an aged person. Then he closed the old person's eyes, turned off the light, left the room, and walked down the hall. As he disappeared down the corridor, the caption read, "*It was the right thing to do—it was the only thing to do.*"

One-half million "unproductive" German people were killed. Eventually, six million Jews were annihilated. Frenzied government officials accepted the philosophy that wholesale human destruction was a solution for establishing Germany's nationalistic and ethnic goals.

One of the observers at the Nuremberg trials was Leo Alexander, a former professor and a psychiatrist now practicing in Newton, Massachusetts. He remained in Germany for several years to research the whole question of how six million human beings could be eliminated without any significant outcry from other citizens. Dr.

Alexander concluded that what happened in Germany began in the early 1930s, when many people were following the Hegelian philosophy of "rational utility," which meant, "what is useful is right."[3] In his article "Medical Science Under Dictatorship" Dr. Alexander explained:

> Irrespective of other ideologic trappings, the guiding philosophic principle of recent dictatorships, including that of the Nazis, has been Hegelian in that what has been considered "rational utility," and corresponding doctrine and planning has replaced moral ethical and religious values. . . .
> Under all forms of dictatorship the dictating bodies or individuals claim that all that is done is being done for the best of people as a whole, and for that reason they look at health merely in terms of utility, efficiency and productivity. It is natural in such a setting that eventually Hegel's principle that "what is useful is good" wins out completely. The killing center is the *reductio ad absurdum* of all health planning based only on rational principles and economy and not on human compassion and divine law.[4]

Therefore, German leaders were figuring out ways to dispense with any human life that wasn't pleasant to look at, wasn't functional, or wasn't productive. And this sinister philosophy was widespread when Adolf Hitler took power. It wasn't much of a step for the dictator to sign decrees empowering his "social executioners" to kill off these people.

In 1935, The Nazi Director of Public Health, Dr. Arthur Guett, wrote in his book *The Structure of Public Health in the Third Reich*:

> The ill-conceived "love of neighbor" has to disappear, especially in relation to inferior or asocial creatures. It is the supreme duty of a national state to grant life and livelihood only to the healthy . . . in order to secure the maintenance of a hereditarily sound and racially pure fold for all eternity. The life of an individual has meaning only in the light of that ultimate aim, that is, in the light of his meaning to his family and to his national state.[5]

Dr. Alexander, in "Medical Science Under Dictatorship" (published *prior* to the 1973 Supreme Court decision) further warned that America was on its way to accepting the Hegelian philosophy.

> To be sure, American physicians are still far from the point of thinking of killing centers, but they have arrived at a danger point in thinking, at which likelihood of full rehabilitation is considered a factor that should determine the amount of time, effort and cost to be devoted to a particular type of patient on the part of the social body upon which this decision rests. At this point Americans should remember that the enormity of a euthanasia movement is present in their own midst.[6]

The Supreme Court Decision

On January 22, 1973, the U.S. Supreme Court ruled (1) that the Fourteenth Amendment's guarantee of personal liberty includes "a right of privacy" broad enough to encompass a woman's personal decision whether or not to terminate her pregnancy; (2) that this right is fundamental and legislation restricting it may be justified only by "a compelling state interest"; and (3) that the state did not demonstrate any such interest, vis-a-vis the unborn, at least prior to viability, because it did not prove that the unborn are "persons" within the Fourteenth Amendment guarantee of a right to live, and because they did not resolve "the difficult question of when life begins."

The Court agreed that if the unborn were considered persons under the Fourteenth Amendment, 'the appellant's case, of course, collapses, for the fetus' right to life is then guaranteed by the Amendment." Instead of making the personhood of the unborn the crux of it's inquiry,

> the Court prejudged the issue by deciding at the threshold that the right of privacy includes a "fundamental right" to abort, i.e., the fetus has no fundamental right to life. In this manner the Court raised a presumption against the unborn's Fourteenth Amendment personhood, and then

made it irreputable by refusing to decide the basic issue of prenatal human beingness.[7]

To put it briefly, the decision nullified all laws against abortion in all fifty states. It authorized the following:

A state may not constitutionally require the consent of a spouse to an abortion during the first trimester.

A state may not constitutionally require the consent of a minor's parent or parents to an abortion during the first trimester.

There are no legal restrictions upon abortion in the first three months.

There are no restrictions in the middle three months except those needed to make the procedure safe for the mother.

Abortion was allowed until birth if one licensed physician judged that it was necessary for the woman's health (defined as ". . . in the light of all factors—physical, emotional, psychological, familial, and the woman's age—relevant to the well being of the patient. All these factors may relate to health"). The U.S. Supreme Court has defined the word "health" to include a broad group of social problems as judged by the mother herself.

What Has the Supreme Court Decision Done to Public Opinion?

One study polled public opinion on abortion before and after the Supreme Court decision. Responses to five virtually identical surveys (1965 and 1972–1975) asking whether or not an abortion is acceptable in six specific situations provided a unique opportunity to evaluate trends in abortion attitudes before and after the Supreme Court Decision of 1973.

Six reasons for abortion were listed on the survey. The first three were "hard" reasons: mothers' health, rape case, and serious defect of the baby. The latter three reasons were "soft" reasons: low income, unmarried, and unwanted. Public support for all six reasons sharply increased after the Court's decision. Before the Supreme Court's decision, nearly half of all respondents did not approve the soft reasons. Afterward, about half of those surveyed approved of abortion for reasons of poverty and nearly all approved the other two soft reasons.[8]

These findings are not surprising. Most people equate legality with morality. Therefore, the moment abortion became legal, in many individuals' minds it became moral and acceptable as well.

Our Society Now

Abortion today is widely accepted as a means of "birth control." Along with the Supreme Court decision, other factors have also influenced this sharp rise of acceptance.

Perhaps second only to the Supreme Court decision is "mass media reinforcement." Mass media reinforcement is necessary to displace the traditional ethic. Although a "new ethic" is developing in our country, the "old" one has yet to be discarded:

> The reverence of each and every human life has been a keystone of western medicine and is the ethic which has caused physicians to try to preserve, protect, repair, prolong, and enhance every human life.
>
> Since the old ethic has not yet been fully displaced, it has been necessary to separate the idea of abortion from the idea of killing which continues to be socially abhorrent. The result has been a curious avoidance of the scientific fact, which everyone really knows, that human life begins at conception, and is continuous, whether intra- or extra-uterine, until death.
>
> The very considerable semantic gymnastics which are required to rationalize abortion as anything but taking a human life would be ludicrous if they were not often put forth under socially impeccable auspices. It is suggested that this schizophrenic sort of subterfuge is necessary because, while a new ethic is being accepted, the old one has not yet been rejected.[9]

Since science verifies that the fetus is indeed a baby, some have found it necessary to instigate a deception of sorts by the use of language. George Orwell pointed out that it is possible to distort language so that words take on the reverse of their actual meaning. "If the words are taken from the language, it can also mean the removal of the concepts they epitomize from people's consciousness."[10] To the average person, "terminate" does not mean the same as to kill. Neither does one automatically think of a baby when the unborn infant is referred to as "fetus," "product of conception," "fetal tissue," "glob of protoplasm," or "fetoplacental unit."

Perhaps a major reason why abortion is viewed lightly is because of what is being passed on as "sex education" in our public schools. I recently saw one of the widely-used sex education films, *A Far Cry From Yesterday* (which H.E.W. recommends for high schools).[11] This is how the order book describes the film:

> *A Far Cry From Yesterday* tells the story of two teenagers who accept an unplanned pregnancy because "they have such a beautiful thing going," without seriously considering the consequences, the near tragic results of their decision: the deterioration of their loving relationship and destruction of their life-styles as the newborn baby demands constant care, responsibility, planning and in short, becomes a "terrible burden." An important film for educating teenagers to make responsible choices in their sexual relationships."

That is the film maker's review. Now I'll share mine. Several scenes have great sociological significance. As I summarize several scenes you'll be better able to understand them.

> *Scene one:*
> When the young girl goes in for "counseling" after finding she's pregnant, this dialogue follows:
>
> Counselor: "Have you told your parents?"
> Girl: "No, it's my problem."
> Counselor: "That's right" (matter-of-factly).

A teenager watching this would easily conclude, "If I get pregnant, it's *my* problem. I shouldn't burden my par-

ents with it." Can you imagine a fourteen-year-old thinking it's not her parents' problem? If she cannot seek counsel and consolation from them, where can she go?

> *Scene two:*
> The counselor continues.
>
> Counselor: "Have you considered abortion?"
> Girl: "I . . . I'm kind of scared about that. I know of a girl
> who hemorrhaged a lot because of it."
>
> The counselor then proceeds to assure her that any compli-
> cation can be taken care of "easily" and concludes with this
> statement, "As a matter of fact, having an abortion in the
> first twelve weeks is actually safer than having a baby."

In this scene, it is significant that the *baby* is never given
any consideration. The girl is afraid that *she* might hem-
orrhage, *not* that she might be taking a human life! Since
the baby is not an issue in this film, adoption is never
mentioned.

Also, of social significance, the next part of the film
shows that although the couple decides to keep the baby,
they are not married. Their living together is brought to
the viewers' attention.

In addition, the couple's premarital sex is never discouraged (the film, instead, discourages the bearing and birth
of a baby). And, because of explicit suggestivity, including
nudity, *A Far Cry From Yesterday* actually encourages sexual promiscuity.

Finally, but perhaps most important, the baby is made
the villain of the film. "We used to laugh a lot before *it*
came along!" "Why the hell did we ever have that kid in
the first place?"

What impressions does this film leave with our young
people? Here are a few. Even if you love each other, and
become sexually intimate, you don't have to consider marriage. It probably would never work out. Also, the first
thing that could destroy your relationship is a baby. And,
don't tell your parents, either. After all, it isn't their prob-

lem. Besides, it's *you* who is important. If pregnancy occurs, get rid of your "problem"; that is the "responsible" thing to do.

And, what about abortion "counseling"? Jack and Barbara Willke said that nowhere among abortion counseling services with which they were familiar were applicants shown a picture of a "fetus" at any of its developing stages. [12] The baby is referred to in the terms of the "coded" words used earlier, i.e., "fetus material." A report on alternatives to abortion included:

> As far as abortion, most adolescents comparable to those in this study could be informed that neither their educational, religious, or social lives nor their economic condition is likely to be adversely affected and that their initial positive feelings about abortion will probably strengthen with the passage of time. [13]

Further on, the author admits that:

> ... for the adolescent who is an applicant for abortion but is ambivalent about it or opposed to termination of pregnancy, the risk of subsequent dissatisfaction appears to be clearly documented. [14]

In reading several pamphlets from various counseling services I was astounded at how they dehumanize the living baby within the mother. One pamphlet, from Planned Parenthood of Memphis, actually had a series of diagrams to illustrate a suction abortion. Next to the second diagram the caption read, "Vacuum suction to remove *pregnancy material.*"

Although many in our society have been duped into believing the baby when intrauterine is a "glob of cells," be assured that the medical profession is not so unenlightened! Dr. Magda Denes, a psychoanalyst from Hungary, did a two year study on abortion, and reported that *every* doctor she interviewed admitted that abortion is the taking of human life. [15] Dr. Mary Kalderone, former medical director of Planned Parenthood says, "of course an abortion is the taking of a human life." Dr. Nevel Sander, who runs a large abortion clinic in Milwaukee said, "Oh, we know it is killing, but the state permits us to kill under certain circumstances, and this is one."

In the years that Father John Powell, one of the leaders of the Pro-Life movement, has been actively debating the pro-life issue, not *one* person who debated with him denied that abortion was the taking of a human life.

The Childless Mother

After extensive research on abortion along with the physical and psychological implications to the women involved, I was amazed by the contradictory conclusions I found. Some were completely opposite of each other. On the one hand, researchers found deep emotional harm (e.g., Aren interviewed 100 randomly selected women about 3 years after abortion and found 23 percent with feelings of severe guilt and 25 percent with mild guilt as the result of abortion). On the other hand, a different set of researchers found no "ill" effects whatsoever, and even a sense of relief following an abortion.

I believe that the psychological effects depend on the woman who has the abortion. Here are some specific examples.

I personally know several women who have had abortions. Two of them do not know that I know. The husband of one asked me privately not to mention the subject of abortion to her because she is so sensitive about it. He said it would upset her terribly. Another woman, who had an abortion, talked to me specifically about it. Upset and ashamed, she could hardly speak. She told me that only two people (including myself) knew about it. At first, she was afraid to tell me because she feared that I would judge her in some way. Actually, I hurt deeply for her. I felt more love for her because she needed it more.

Father John Powell shares this experience with a former pupil, "Teresa," who had gotten an abortion. She talked at length about it. Teresa had such strong convictions about it, even before doing it, that she asked the nurse at the clinic for some water to pour over her stomach so the baby would be baptized. She was told to "shut up!" Then at Teresa's side another young applicant for abortion explained why she was having hers. Since she had a ski trip planned at Aspen, she wasn't going to let a pregnancy interfere with it. A human life and a ski trip: there was no doubt in this young woman's mind—get rid of the baby! Teresa put her hands over her ears.

Father Powell talked to Teresa about God's healing and forgiveness and expressed his personal love for her. But he says that he'll never forget one of the last things Teresa said to him as she left: "You know, I knew when I was in college that I was a liar and a cheat, and a manipulator, and a flirt. And I know a lot of things about myself—I could live with those. I don't know if I can live with this."[16]

Another girl whom he counseled said, "Of course, I'll remember. Two years from now when I see a two-year-old, I'll remember—that's how old my baby would have been, and four years from now. . . ."[17] From her two-year study of an abortion clinic, Magda Denes cites a young mother who aborted a live fetus:

> The mother delivered when there was no one there, and there was some period when the mother was holding the baby . . . and it was grabbing on to her.[18]

This young girl will bear the memory of her dying baby throughout the rest of her life. How could she live in peace with this experience etched in her consciousness? A wise psychiatrist said, "It is easier to scrape the baby from the womb than it is to scrape its memory from the mother's mind."

The World Health Organization, in an official statement

in 1970, said: "serious mental disorders arise more often in women with previous mental problems. Thus the very women for whom legal abortion is considered justified on psychiatric grounds are the ones who have the highest risk of postabortion disorders."

One of the more alarming aspects of the Supreme Court decision is allowing *minors* to get abortions without parental consent. Legally, a thirteen-year-old girl may, without parental consent, make this major decision that will affect her entire life.

In many high schools, if a girl thinks she's pregnant, she may take a urinalysis test at school. If the test results show that she's pregnant, she may check in with the school health office, go out for an abortion, come back by the end of the day, and go home—without her parent's knowledge.

By contrast, other women don't seem to be negatively affected at all. "Positive sequelae to abortion were studied by Osofsky and Osofsky, who established that relief was the predominant emotional response in a sample of 250 women requesting legal abortion."[19]

For this very reason, the doctor who led the crusade to legalize abortion, Bernard Nathanson, began to question the morality of it. While preparing an article on the success of the abortion clinic he was running (the busiest licensed abortion facility in the western world), he read the questionnaires that women, mostly young, filled out. He said, "I couldn't help but be disturbed by the fact that the only emotion they seemed to express about their abortions was relief. No remorse, no regret, no sense of loss among 26,000 women. I found that a little alarming."[20]

Billy Jean King was about to enter a tennis tournament, worth twenty-thousand dollars for the final winner, when she discovered she was pregnant. She got rid of her baby and publicly encouraged women to "follow her example." One girl that Father Powell counseled said that when she told her boyfriend she was pregnant, he retorted, "Get rid of the kid—it's like using a vacuum cleaner. I'll pay for half." Father Powell commented that he could tell by her body language that it really didn't bother her. "If *that* doesn't bother you," he thought, "*What would?*"[21]

Doctors as well as young women have become anesthetized to emotional sensitivity and moral integrity. Dr. Bernard Nathanson said of his own feelings,

> I began to worry about where my psyche was going because like everyone else involved, staff and patients both, I was treating these abortions, these mini-tragedies, only as industrial statistics.[22]

Author Magda Denes shares further examples.[23] One doctor, after stating emphatically that he had no doubt he was killing a live baby in performing an abortion, said,

> ... so I can imagine if I had started doing twenty-four-weekers right off the bat, I would have had much greater conflict in my own mind whether this was tantamount to murder. But since we started gradually with fifteen–sixteen weekers ... the fetus never got consideration.

Another doctor, in the same clinic, stated,

> You have to become a bit schizophrenic. In one room you encourage the patient that the slight irregularity of the fetal heart is not important, everything is going well, and she is going to have a nice baby; and then you shut the door and go into the next room and assure another patient on whom you just did a saline abortion, that it's fine if the heart is already irregular, she has nothing to worry about, she is not going to have a live baby. ... I have no trouble making that switch.

What About the Babies?

There is no doubt among doctors and scientists that the "being" within a mother's womb is a live baby. One of the most distinguished scientific meetings of the last decade that considered this question in depth was the First International Conference on Abortion, held in Washington, D.C., in October, 1976. It brought together authorities from around the world in the fields of medicine, law, ethics, and the social sciences. The first major question considered by the medical group (composed of biochemists, geneticists, professors of obstetrics and gynecology) was, "When does human life begin?" Their nearly unanimous conclusion was:

> The majority of the group could find no point in time between the union of sperm and egg, or at least the blasto-cyst stage and the birth of the infant at which point we could say that this was not a human life.

Jack and Barbara Willke agree: "It is not a potential human being. It is, rather, a human being with vast potential."[24]

How are these human beings, these babies, aborted? Five procedures of induced abortions include: 1) Suction aspiration; 2) Dilatation and curettage; 3) Prostaglandin; 4) Salt poisoning; and 5) Hysterotomy. With the suction method, the surgeon stretches the cervical muscle ring open and inserts into the uterus a hollow plastic tube with a knife-like edge on the tip. The suction tears the baby into pieces. The surgeon then cuts the deeply-rooted placenta from the inner wall of the uterus. The scraps are sucked out into a bottle.

A "D & C" is similar to the suction procedure except that the surgeon inserts a curette (a loop-shaped steel knife) into the uterus. With this, the unborn baby and placenta is cut into pieces and scraped out into a basin. Bleeding is usually profuse.

Prostaglandin (Prostin F2 Alpha), when it works, pro-duces labor and delivery at any stage of pregnancy. If the baby is old enough to survive the trauma of labor, it will likely be born alive, but is usually too small to survive.

The saline poisoning method is done after the sixteenth week. A large needle containing concentrated salt solution is injected through the abdominal wall into the amniotic fluid. The baby swallows it, is poisoned, struggles, and sometimes convulses. It takes more than an hour to kill the baby. When this method is successful, the mother goes into labor about one day later and delivers a dead baby. A few of these babies are still alive at birth. These are sometimes referred to as "candy apple babies" because the corrosive effect of the concentrated salt often burns and strips away the entire outer layer of the baby's skin. It is probably every bit as painful as napalm. One doctor noticed that at the time of saline infusion "there was a lot of activity in the uterus. That's obviously the fetus being distressed by swallowing the concentrated salt solution and kicking violently . . . the death trauma."[25]

A hysterotomy is like a caesarean section. The mother's abdomen is surgically opened, as is her uterus. The baby is then lifted out and discarded. Almost all hysterotomy babies are born alive.

> The "Stophill Hospital baby" in Glasgow was aborted by this technique. This child was carried from the operating theatre in a paper disposal bag, and left in the snow outside the porter's lodge for about 30 minutes until the Porter picked it up to throw it into the incinerator. He was about to do so when he heard the baby cry. He rushed it back to the theatre [surgical room] where it was resuscitated and despite bad head injuries survived for hours. Subsequently a public inquiry was carried out but no action could be brought against those involved because they had been acting "legally." On responding to the procurator's suggestion that a baby aborted "alive" should be resuscitated, the pathologist to whom he addressed the remark replied that "this would defeat the purpose of the abortion act." The purpose of the English Abortion Law is to insure that these children do not survive.[26]

Until April of 1974, when the House of Representatives voted to prohibit research on a human fetus, human fetal experimentation was carried on in this country.

> Dr. A. Ammann of the University of California planted human fetal thymus glands into two older children. Both donor humans were killed.[27]

> Dr. R. Goodlin at Stanford University, California, did experiments including "slicing open the rib cage of a still-living human fetus in order to observe the heart action.... Some as old as twenty-four weeks... were used."[28]

Human fetal experimentation still occurs in many countries. How can this happen? Too easily, as Jack and Barbara Willke comment: "Once reverence for life is lost at any stage of human life, practices like this soon appear.[29]

What About "Defective Children?"

> The assumption that handicapped people enjoy life less than "normal" [people] has recently been shown to be false. A well documented investigation has shown that there is no difference between malformed and normal persons in their degree of life satisfaction, outlook of what lies immediately ahead, and vulnerability to frustration.[30]

In a testimony before the Ohio Legislature in 1971, Rosalie Craig said, "There has not been a single organization of parents of mentally retarded children that has ever endorsed abortion. We, who are parents of these children and have borne the burden ask that before you, the legislatures, propose to speak for us, by possibly authorizing abortion for fetal abnormality, please ask our opinion first."[31]

A close friend of mine who gave birth to a little girl with a handicap told me recently, "I believe that the Lord brought my little girl into the world for what she could do for other people. She brings out something special in other people—character qualities they may not even know they have. But she has been a special blessing to me."

And what about the "unwanted" babies, born with deformities or deficiencies previously undetected? During a commencement program at Wheaton College, Dr. C. Everett Koop (Surgeon-in-Chief, Children's Hospital,

Philadelphia) made ten predictions of what the liberal Supreme Court abortion decision would do to our country. His eighth prediction was, "The newborn infant who is not perfect is probably the next target." His prediction has already been supported. Typical of advocates for restricted infanticide is Dr. James Watson, codiscoverer of the double helix, the master molecule DNA. He commented:

> If a child were not declared alive until three days after birth, then all parents could be allowed the choice that only a few are given under the present system. . . . The doctor could allow the child to die if the parents so chose and save a lot of misery and suffering.[32]

Also, this sobering observation was recently published:

> The Christian conscience is becoming increasingly dulled in the face of today's propaganda. I just read about a proposed seminar entitled "Permissible and Disputed Means of Infanticide." Is it shocking or are people aware that in hospitals today *as many* defective babies are allowed to die as were aborted ten years ago?[33]

A Biblical Viewpoint

From cover to cover, the Bible affirms that life is precious to God. When the Word of God speaks of man in the womb it does so as it speaks of the sweep of God's sovereignty from creation to the end of time.

> This is what the Lord says—he who made you, who formed you in the womb, and who will help you. . . ." "This is what the Lord says—your Redeemer, who formed you in the womb: I am the Lord, who has made all things, who alone stretched out the heavens, who spread out the earth by myself (Isa. 44:2,24).

Other Scripture references include: ". . . you brought me forth from my mother's womb" (Ps. 71:6); "Sons are a heritage from the Lord; children a reward from him" (Ps.

127:3); and "For you created my inmost being; you knit me together in my mother's womb." But, to me, the one that really stands out is found in the first chapter of Jeremiah: "The Word of the Lord came to me saying, *before I formed you in the womb, I knew you* [italics mine], before you were born I set you apart; I appointed you as a prophet to the nations" (Jer. 1:5).

A young woman sitting in a doctor's office waiting to have an abortion, picked up a Gideon Bible and began reading, searching for some comfort. In this desperate hour of her life she found more than comfort: she found the person of Jesus Christ, who said, "I will be with you always, to the very end of the age" (Matt. 28:20). She became assured that God could give her a peace that passes all understanding. She broke her appointment and walked out, never to return. Today, as she gives her testimony of what Christ can mean in a life, she holds the hand of her beautiful three-year-old daughter.

Conclusion

> Even if a majority of citizens did favor legalization, and I think it does not, convictions so deep as those of the opponents of abortion must be taken into account if they are not to be wholly alienated from the body politic. The fact that no one who does not believe in abortion will be forced to engage in abortion (as yet) does not help. It is like telling someone in Nazi Germany, "Don't worry, your hands are clean, you don't have to guard the camps." In order to go on supporting a government which he thinks kills the innocent, a person must surely begin to lose whatever moral standards he has.... At least one New York Senator refused to agree to any aspect of a new budget as long as it contained money "to kill babies."[34]

Dr. John Kelley of Chicago, who later moved to Ireland, said, "How do you remain an innocent bystander at murder?" Part of his tax money was being used for abortions for the poor.

Do you know that American taxpayers have paid for one third of more than six million abortions? In Washington, D.C., where there were more abortions than live births, federal taxes paid for 85 percent of those abortions.

What can you do? Here are ways you can advance the pro-life movement in our country:[35]

1. *Pray.*
2. *Educate*—both yourself and others about the truths concerning the abortion issue.
3. *Work*—get involved in one of the Pro-life organizations, i.e., Birthright, Right to Life, etc.
4. *Contribute*—not only time and energy, but financially if possible.
5. *Vote*—be aware of where candidates stand on the abortion issue and vote accordingly. Also work for those whose views are pro-life.
6. *Write*—to National Legislators, State and local representatives, newspapers, television... make them precise, polite, and brief, and always sign your name.
7. *Love them*—love the precious babies who will never see the light of life; feel the gentle touch of another human being; and love the mothers, many of whom will never forget their aborted babies. Love them with God's love, which is unconditional.

Linda Burnett

Psychiatric Comment

To become a psychiatrist, I first had to complete enough medical training to become a family physician. Consequently, I have delivered babies, observed (but refused to perform) abortions, and sat in on abortion boards who decided which young women have "medical grounds" for abortions. As a psychiatrist, I since have counseled scores of women whose guilt feelings stem from abortions they have had.

Recently, I discharged from our psychiatry ward an intelligent, college-educated, attractive woman in her early thirties whose suicidal depression was caused by guilt feelings from abortions she had gotten years earlier. She, Mrs. K., had almost totally repressed her guilt feelings and was apparently living a normal, depression-free life. Then an elderly, senile man approached her eight-year-old daughter sexually, but did not rape her. This, of course, would upset any mother. Any normal mother would be angry at the old man, even though senile, and see to it that he was kept in better custody. Any normal mother would be concerned about her eight-year-old daughter and counsel her to be sure the girl talked about her feelings.

But this mother *over-reacted* to the situation by rapidly developing a psychotic (out-of-touch with reality) depressive reaction and made a serious attempt at suicide. I saw her in the emergency room, where she was spared from self-inflicted death, and persuaded her to come to our psychiatry ward when she recovered physically from the suicide attempt.

Even before getting her history, it seemed obvious to me that her suicidal reaction could have stemmed from repressed but severe guilt feelings. I assumed also that these guilt feelings likely involved sexual guilt of some sort, since the incident with her daughter unleashed her repressed guilt.

I was right. But when I first asked Mrs. K whether she had any sexual guilt feelings from her past, such as from an affair or an abortion, she denied it. A well-read woman, she could quote popular opinion to defend herself from repressed guilt resulting from two abortions. After further gentle probing, she became bitterly aware of the guilt feelings she had repressed, and wept profusely. I encouraged her to pray for God's forgiveness for what she had done and then persuaded her to forgive herself. Within two weeks of daily therapy, she was able to work through her guilt, get over her suicidal thoughts, and gain more joy in her life than she had experienced in years.

Mrs. K's condition is not isolated, and similar experiences are extremely common. During my psychiatric training, my pro-abortion professors admitted in their lectures and private conversations that the psychological problems that result from having an abortion are as frequent and severe as the psychological problems that result from giving birth to an unwanted baby (whether from giving it up for adoption or from keeping it). Justifying an abortion with the psychological jargon—"to prevent psychological damage to the mother" is a well known farce. It's voiced in hospitals and clinics merely to encourage the mother *legally* to do what she wants to do. In none of the abortion boards I observed was it any more than a formality. In none of them was it obvious that the psychiatrist really believed in his heart that having the abortion would be less psychologically damaging than other alternatives. It was merely granting legal permission to the mother. I frequently heard the rationalization, "Well . . . better that she get a 'clean' abortion in the hospital than a 'dirty' abortion in the streets."

That "clean" abortions are safe and without complications is mere folklore. The risks are definitely played down. In a medical journal, Dr. J. A. Stallworthy and his associates state:

> There has been almost a conspiracy of silence in declaring its risks. Unfortunately, because of emotional reaction to legal abortion, well-documented evidence from countries with a vast experience of it receives little attention in either the medical or daily press. This is medically indefensible when patients suffer as a result. For these reasons we summarize the facts of our experience of Obstetrics and Gynecology. We are proud neither of the number of pregnancies which have been terminated nor the complications described.
>
> In the experience of this English-teaching hospital there was a 27 percent complication rate from infection, 9.5 percent needed transfusions, 5 percent of suction and D & C abortions tore the cervical muscle, and 1.7 percent perforated. It is significant that some of the more serious com-

plications occurred with the most senior and experienced operators.

These complications are seldom mentioned by those who claim that abortion is safe.[36]

Americans are mislead by liberals both in and out of the medical profession. *Millions* of *live* fetuses are being killed in America to form a significant portion of the unwanted generation. Those who disagree are oppressed. I was scared of getting "flunked" or into serious trouble in medical school when I refused to assist with abortions or to approve them while sitting on "abortion boards." It definitely angered some of my superiors, even though I was extremely polite and accepted their right to have an opinion that differed from mine.

My only consolation is my belief that some of these millions of aborted babies may be better off than those who join the unwanted generation in the world that exists outside of the womb. I believe that aborted babies go to be with God in heaven and will live eternally as adult beings within a loving spiritual family. When King David's baby died, he stated with firm hope that someday he would be happily reunited with his baby. As a medical doctor who has delivered babies, I can't imagine that God would have one redemptive policy for babies fed on the breast but another fate for babies fed through the mother's umbilical cord.

Paul Meier, M.D.

Notes

1. Father John Powell, S. J., Speech given at a "Faith at Work" conference in Gatlinburg, Tenn., 1978.
2. Jack and Barbara Willke, *Handbook of Abortion* (Cincinnati: Hayes Publishing Co., 1971–1975), p. 139.

3. "A German philosopher by the name of Hegel (1770–1831) attacked the idea of absolute moral value with the notion that men with competing views of morality (thesis vs. antithesis) can by rational processes arrive at a synthesis, an agreement based on utility or usefulness. As life goes on and situations and the needs of people change, yesterday's synthesis becomes the thesis to another antithesis out of which comes forth a new synthesis, or agreement. Hegel's basic idea is that the center of morality's circle is not fixed; it keeps moving as situations keep changing. Yesterday's wrong becomes today's right. New ethics replace old ethics. Killing innocent human beings was wrong yesterday, but today it is no longer socially abhorrent" (Clifford E. Bajema, *Abortion and the Meaning of Personhood* [Grand Rapids: Baker Book House, 1974] pp. 7–8).

4. Leo Alexander, "Medical Science Under Dictatorship," *The New England Journal of Medicine* 241, no. 2 (July 1949): 46.

5. Arthur Guett, *The Structure of Public Health in the Third Reich.* Cited in materials on abortion by Robert L. Sassone.

6. Alexander, "Medical Science Under Dictatorship," p. 46.

7. R. M. Bryn, "The New Jurisprudence," *Journal of American Medical Association*, 27 July 1976, pp. 359–360.

8. W. R. Arney and W. H. Trescher, "Trends in Attitudes Toward Abortion," *Family Planning Perspectives* 8 (May–June 1976): 117.

9. *Journal of the California State Medical Association*, September 1970, cited by Willke, *Handbook on Abortion*, p. 37.

10. Willke, *Handbook on Abortion*, p. 197.

11. *A Far Cry From Yesterday*, Film no. 1022 (Tucson: Planned Parenthood of Southern Arizona).

12. Willke, *Handbook on Abortion*, p. 197.

13. J. I. Rosoff, "Pregnancy Counseling and Abortion Referral for Patients in Federally Funded Family Planning Programs," *Family Planning Perspectives*, 8 (January–February 1976): 43–46.

14. Ibid.

15. Magda Denes, *In Necessity and Sorrow: Life and Death in an Abortion Hospital* (New York: Penguin Books, Inc., 1977). Throughout the entire book she relates interviewing different doctors and never encountered one who said abortion wasn't murder.

16. Powell, Speech in Gatlinburg, Tenn.

17. Ibid.

18. Denes, *In Necessity and Sorrow*, p. 79.

19. Ellen W. Freeman, "Influence of Personality Attributes on Abortion Experiences," *American Journal of Orthopsychiatry*, July 1977, pp. 503–508.

20. Charles and Bonnie Remsberg, "Second Thoughts on Abortion from the Doctor Who Led the Crusade for It," *Good Housekeeping*, March 1976, p. 69.

21. Powell, Speech in Gatlinburg, Tenn.

22. Remsberg, "Second Thoughts on Abortion."

23. Denes, *In Necessity and Sorrow,* pp. 68, 69.

24. Willke, *Handbook on Abortion,* p. 16.

25. Denes, *In Necessity and Sorrow,* p. 68.

26. Willke, *Handbook on Abortion,* pp. 32–33.

27. Ibid., p. 128.

28. Ibid.

29. Ibid., 130.

30. Ibid., pp. 118–119.

31. Ibid., p. 117.

32. *Time,* 28 May 1973.

33. W. F. Sullivan, "Working Together for Christ: Facing the Anti-Life Challenge," *Hospital Progress,* May 1977, pp. 82–84.

34. Richard Stith, *Commonwealth,* 12 November 1971.

35. Adapted from Willke, *Handbook on Abortion,* pp. 200–201.

36. J. A. Stallworthy et al., "Legal Abortion: A Critical Assessment of Its Risks," *The Lancet,* 4 December 1971.

11

P.S. to Fathers

It's late and I'm tired. But my heart is full of gratitude to God for my husband, Bill. And so I feel led to start my "P.S. to Fathers" chapter.

Today has been a good day. I had some time to rest and some time to myself—just to be myself and not only "mama" to two youngsters.

This "holiday" became possible for me because Bill took John Mark on an outing while I napped, and later he took both boys to the store while I just primped—I actually had some "nothing-to-do" time on my hands.

Yesterday I saw one of the sweetest scenes I've ever witnessed, and I'm sure it will be etched forever in my memory. Bill headed out the door with his fishing pole and gear, and right behind him trailed our three-year-old, Brian, with his toy fishing pole. He was so excited to be going fishing with daddy. Although they were gone only an hour-and-a-half, Brian knew that he was "daddy's little man."

I found out two weeks ago that I am pregnant again. It was definitely unexpected, and, I must admit, I cried much of the day. But weighing the added responsibility this would bring, God's peace, which passes all understanding, encompassed me and has remained.

One reason I'm not "panicky" at the thought of having three children under four years old is that I can rely on Bill when I need him. As my provider and protector, Bill is sensitive to my emotional, as well as physical needs. Knowing that Bill will be home when he can be, that he understands my needs, and that he wants to help is half the battle.

Perhaps one reason why he is so helpful is that I am honest with him about my needs. And, I have told him that never in my life will I need him more, as we progress through the years, than I need him now.

Someday I will look back with loving memories and much gratitude, and say to myself, "How blessed I was that Bill was there when I needed him the most. Praise God, he understood and cared enough to meet my emotional and physical needs when they were greatest."

Unfortunately, this was not the case for many of my friends. I have a fifty-five-year-old friend whose husband became a Christian just a few years ago, and he treats her like a queen. As we were having lunch one day, I told her how lucky I thought she was. "Oh, he's good to me all right," she told me, "but I never *saw* him when the girls were little, and then I needed him the most."

Another friend, who is in her thirties, is half of a couple known as "Bob and Betty Bliss." They appear to have the ideal marriage. But, in talking to her one day, I was surprised to hear her say, "You know, Linda, my husband wasn't always this thoughtful. In fact, when I needed him the most—when our boys were little—I had to raise them on my own. He never did anything to help me."

Although I sense that these women have forgiven their husbands for their lack of love (Christ said that husbands should love their wives as He loved the church and *gave* Himself for her), they will never *forget* that when they needed them the most—and only a mother can know how desperate that need can be—their husbands didn't meet that dire need. Sadly, this may be "scar tissue" that will remain with these women throughout their lives. I feel, however, that if they give these "wounds" to Christ, He will heal them and help these women focus on today and on the love they can experience now.

Fathers, until now you may have been looking through "a glass darkly." You may not realize how much your wife needs you right now. Take my word for it. The best way that you can love that woman in your life is to be available to help her.

And the rewarding part is knowing you are not only meeting your wife's needs, but at the same time you can meet the deep needs of your children—their need to be loved in that special way that only a daddy can provide. The only way to establish a relationship is to spend time with someone. That goes for your children as well as other adults. This building of a relationship must start from infancy. You can't just walk up to a five-year-old and say, "Now, let's be friends."

Bill already has such a relationship with Brian, three, and John Mark, one-and-a-half. I am sometimes a bit jealous in that they are both "daddy's boys."

Someone once asked Bill, "What if your sons turn out bad?" He replied, "I'm going to be the best father I know how, and discipline them the way the Lord would have me do it, and spend as much time with them as I feel I should. Then I will have no regrets, and I'll know that I did everything that I could for them. But I'm not worried about that because I have God's promise that if I train them up in the way that they should go *they will not depart from it.*"

Is there any other way for a father to live? Bill and I have no fear of the future, and we will have few regrets about the past.

Linda Burnett

Psychiatric Comment

I usually can talk to an adult counselee ten or twenty minutes and guess accurately how much time the father spent with the counselee during childhood. The voice, body language, and self-concept all reflect it. I have asked many highly-regarded older men what they would change if they could live their lives over. Most of these men are strong Christian leaders. Almost without exception, they said they would have spent a little less time doing "Christian work" and more time with their own children. God's Word tells us that if any Christian man doesn't meet the needs of his own family, he is worse than an unbeliever (cf. 1 Tim. 5:8). God never calls any Christian father to do anything that would detract significantly from his *daily* child-rearing duties. The effects on children of *father absence* or *passivity* (if the father is present) are devastating.

My goal with my own children is to spend one or two hours communicating with them (or playing with them) each weekday and two to four hours each weekend day. On the average, I will allow myself to be gone one or two evenings each week and no more than one weekend per month. Later in life, I may look back and think this wasn't sufficient time, but I'm listening to the wisdom of my older friends. I'm spending much more time with my four children than I would have if I had not seen, in my psychiatric practice, so many bad results of father absence. The quantity of time spent with children is just as important as the quality of time.

At times, being with my four children can be frustrating. Sometimes I am irritated by their griping and squabbling. But I have to admit, my involvement in my children's lives is by far the most profitable investment I could ever have made. My wife and children are my primary reasons for existing. They are my highest calling from God.

Paul Meier, M.D.

Bibliography

Day-Care

Allen, Winifred Y., and Campbell, Doris. *The Creative Nursery Center, A Unified Service to Children and Parents.* New York: Family Service Association of America, 1948.

Annas, G. J. "Let Them Eat Cake." *Hastings Center Report,* August, 1977.

Auerbach, Stevanne, and Rivaldo, James A. "Child Care: A Comprehensive Guide: 11 Model Programs and Their Components. *Human Sciences* 21 (1976).

Auerbach, Stevanne. "Pre-School Push to Independence." *Parents Magazine,* December 1977, p. 334.

Augrist, Shirley, et al. "How Working Mothers Manage: Socioeconomic Difference in Work, Child Care and Household Tasks." *Social Science Quarterly,* March, 1976

Beer, Ethel S. *Working Mothers and the Day Nursery.* Mystic, Conn.: Lawrence Verry, Inc., 1977.

———. *The Day Nursery.* New York: E. P. Dutton, 1943.

Bergstrom, Joan L., and Gold, Jane R. "Day Care and Child Development." *Sweden's Day Nurseries: Focus on Programs for Infants and Toddlers.* Mt. Rainer, Maryland: Daycare and Child Development Council of America, n.d.

———. "How to Find Reliable Day Care." *Changing Times,* 1978, p. 28.

Billante, G. W. "On-the-Job Training for Motherhood: Child Observation Nursery." *Parents Magazine,* August 1976, p. 36–38.

Blehar, Mary Curtis. "Anxious Attachment and Defensive Reactions Association With Day-Care." *Child Development* 45 (1974): 691.

Black, R. E., et al. "Giardiasis in Day-Care Centers: Evidence of Person to Person Transmission." *Pediatrics* 60 (October 1977): 486–491.

Bowlby, John. *Child Care and the Growth of Love*. Baltimore: Penguin Books, 1965.

Bowley, Agatha H. *Children At Risk*. New York: Churchill Livingston, 1975.

Boyd, Marjorie. "The Case Against Day Care." *The Washington Monthly*, 1976, p. 22.

Brown, F., et al. "Childhood Bereavement and Subsequent Crime." *British Journal of Psychiatry* 112 (1966): 1048.

Bruch, Hilda. "Family Transactions in Eating Disorders." *Comprehensive Psychiatry* 12 (1972): 238–248.

"Child Rearing: The Day-Care Controversy." *Science Digest*, June 1976, pp. 8–9.

Conn, D. "Kids and Kamaras: Program at the Morning Sunday and Free School in New Haven." *Popular Photography*, January 1977, p. 564.

Curtis, J. "Child Care Alternatives." *Harper's Bazaar*, October 1977, p. 1774.

Daly, L. I. M. "Nursery School Co-op: A Design to Delight Small Fry, Plainview." *Better Homes and Gardens*, March 1975, pp. 66–67.

David, Miriam, and Lezine, Irene. "Early Child Care in France." *Early Child Development and Care*, 1974, p. 148.

"Day Care Children: No Ill Effects." *Science News*, 18 February 1976, pp. 133–134.

De Leon, Shirley. "Verdict on Nursery Schools: Big on Promises, Short on Delivery." *Parents Magazine*, May 1975, pp. 34–35.

"Dilemma for Working Mothers: Not Enough Day Care Centers." *U.S. News & World Report*, 12 April 1976, pp. 49–50.

Eagle, G. "My Fight to Become the Fullest Full-Time Mother: Management of Day-Care Center." *Redbook*, June 1976, p. 474.

Earhart, Eileen M. "Implementation of Attention and Classification Curriculum in Day-Care and Early Childhood Centers." *Child Care Quarterly*, Winter 1974, pp. 225–236.

Einklestein, Ellen. "The Development of a Systematic Method by Which Day Care Staff can Select Gestural Imitation Curriculum Procedures for Individual Infants." *Child Study Journal*, 1974, pp. 169–178.

Evans, Belle E.; Shub, Beth; and Weinstein, Marilyn. *Day Care: How to Plan, Develop and Operate a Day Care Center*. Boston: Beacon Press, 1971.

Evans, Belle E. *Designing a Day-Care Center: How to Select, Design and Develop a Day-Care Center*. Boston: Beacon Press, 1974.

Evans, Sue, et al. "Failure to Thrive: A Study of 45 Children and Their Families." *Journal of the American Academy of Child Psychology* 11 (1972): 440–457.

Fandetti, Donald V. "Day Care in Working Class Ethnic Neighborhoods: Implications for Social Policy." *Child Welfare*, November 1976, pp. 618–626.

Farran, Dale, and Ramey, Craig. "Infant Day Care and Attachment Behaviors Toward Mothers and Teachers." *Child Development*, September 1977, pp. 1112–1116.

Fein, Greta, and Clarke-Stewart, Alison. *Day Care in Context*. New York: John Wiley & Sons, 1973.

Franklin, A. A. "Finding Child Care When Mother Works." *Parents Magazine*, October 1975, pp. 124.

Gold, Delores, and Andres, David. "Maternal Employment and Child Development at Three Age Levels." *Journal of Research and Development in Education* 10 (1977).

Goldman, Joyce. "Vacuum Packed Day Care." *Ms*, March 1975, p. 81.

Goldman, P. S. "The Relationship Between the Amount of Stimulation in Infancy and Subsequent Emotionality." *Annals of the New York Academy of Science* 159 (1969): 681–695.

Gonzales, Gustavo. "The Identification of Competencies Desirable in Teachers Working with Pre-school Chicano Children." *Journal of Instructional Psychology*, Summer 1975, pp. 15–18.

Grambs, Jean Dresden, ed. "Working Mothers—the Wonder Women," *Parents Magazine*, April 1977, p. 33.

Harlow, Harry F., and Harlow, Margaret, K. *The Affectional System in Behavior of Non-Human Primates*. Edited by H M. Schrier, et al. vol. 2. New York: Academy Press, 1965.

Harrell, Janet. F., and Ridley, Carl A. "Substitute Child Care, Maternal Employment and the Quality of Mother–Child Interaction." *Journal of the Marriage and the Family*, August 1975, p. 556.

Haskins, Ron; Farran, Dale; and Sanders, Joseph. "Making the Day Care Decision." *Parents Magazine*, April 1978, p. 58.

Hojlund, Louise. "What We Say and Do When We Deal with Children." *Skolepsycologi* 12 (1975): 84–96.

Honig, Alice S. "Curriculum for Infants in Day Care." *Child Welfare* 53 (1974): 633–642.

"Impact on the Home When Mother Takes a Job." *U.S. News & World Report*, 15 January 1979.

"Ingredients of a Creative Family Day Care." *Child Welfare*, February 1975.

Johnson, Harriet Merrill. *School Begins at 2:00*. New York: Agathon Press, 1970.

Kagan, Jerome. "All About Day Care." *Parents Magazine*, April 1977, pp. 40–44.

Kagan, Jerome, and Bush, S. "Day Care Is as Good as Home Care." *Psychology Today*, May 1976, pp. 36–37.

Kaufman, I. C., et al. "Effects of Separation from Mother on the Emotional Behavior of Infant Monkeys." *Annals of the New York Academy of Science* 159 (1969): 681–695.

Kelly, M. "How to Find a Nurse for Your Child." *Harper's Bazaar*, August 1976, p. 854.

Keniston, K., and Tucker, G. "Citizens Who Need Us Most." *Saturday Review*. September 1977, p. 560.

Kerserling, Mary Dublin. "A Report Based on Findings of the National Council of Jewish Women." *Windows on Day Care*. New York: National Council of Jewish Women, n.d.

Kogelschatz, Joan L.; Adams, Paul L.; and Tucker, Daniel. "Family Styles of Fatherless Households." *Journal of the American Academy of Child Psychiatry* 11 (1972): 356–383.

Krell, Robert. "Problems of the Single-Parent Family Unit." *Canadian Medical Association Journal* 107 (1972): 867–868.

Laosa, Luis M. "Child Care and the Culturally Different Child." *Child Care Quarterly* 3 (1974): 214–224.

Levitan, Sara, and Alderman, Karen Cleary. *Child Care and ABC's Too*. Baltimore: Johns Hopkins University Press, 1975.

MacRae, John, and Jackson, Herbert. "Are Behavioral Effects of Infant Day-Care Program Specific?" *Developmental Psychology* 12 (May 1976): 269–270.

Martensson, S. "Childhood Interaction and Temporal Organization." *Economic Geography*, April 1977, pp. 99–125.

McCutcheon, B., and Calhoun, K. S. "Social and Emotional Adjustments of Infants and Toddlers to a Day-Care Setting." *American Journal of Orthopsychology*, January 1976, pp. 104–108.

McDanald, Eugene. "Emotional Growth of the Child." *Texas Medicine* 63 (1967): 74.

McDonald, Geraldine. "Educational Innovation: The Case of the New Zealand Playcentre." *New Zealand Journal of Educational Studies*, November 1974, pp. 153–165.

McGrew, William Clement. *An Ethological Study of Children's Behavior*. New York: Academic Press, 1972.

Melzack, R. "The Role of Early Experience in Emotional Arousal." *Annals of the New York Academy of Science* 159 (1969): 721.

Nagera, Humberto. "Day-Care Centers: Red Light, Green Light, or Amber Light." *International Review of Psycho-Analysis* 2 (1975): 121–137.

Neubauer, Peter, et al. *Early Child Day Care*. New York: Jason Aronson, 1974.

Norman, Marjorie. "Substitutes for Mother." *Human Behavior*, February 1978, pp. 18–22.

Pappenfort, Donnell M., and Morgan, Dee. *Child Caring, Social Policy and the Institution*. Chicago: Aldine Publishing Co., 1973.

Peters, John E. *Lectures on Piaget*. Little Rock: University of Arkansas Child Study Center, 1973.

Peters, Roger, and Torrance, Paul E. "Effects of Triadic Interaction on Performance of Five-Year-Old Disadvantaged Children." *Psychology Reports*, June 1973, p. 41.

Porterfield, Janet; Jackson, Herbert; Risley, Emily; and Todd, R. "Contingent Observation: An Effective and Acceptable Procedure for Reducing Disruptive Behavior of Young Children in a Group Setting." *Journal of Applied Behavior Analysis*, Spring 1976, pp. 55–64.

Prescott, Elizabeth, and Jones, Elizabeth. *Day Care as a Child Rearing Environment*. Washington: National Association for the Education of Young Children, 1972.

Prescott, Elizabeth; Milich, Cynthia; and Jones, Elizabeth. *The Politics of Day Care*. Washington: National Association for the Education of Young Children, 1972.

Pringle, Mia, and Naidoo, Sandhya. "Early Child Care in Britain." *Early Child Development and Care*, 1974, pp. 299–473.

Readiman, Florence, A. *Child Care and Working Mothers: A Study of Arrangements Made for Day Time Care for Children*. New York: Child Welfare League of America, 1968.

Riskind, Mary L. "Play/Learn or Pre-school." *Mothers*, September–October 1978, p. 48.

Robertson, James, and Robertson, Joyce "Young Children in Brief Separation: A Fresh Look." *The Psychoanalytic Study of the Child*. Edited by Ruth S. Eissler, vol. 26. New Haven: Yale University Press, 1972.

Roby, Pamela "Child Care—Who Cares?" *Foreign and Domestic Infant and Early Childhood Development Policies*. New York: Basic Books, 1973.

Rodriguez, Dorothy, and Hignett, William F. "Guidelines for the Selection of Home-Based Day Caregivers." *Child Welfare*, 55, no. 1 (January 1976) 120–26.

Ross, Andrew, and Schrieber, Lawrence J. "O. H. Bellefaire's Day Treatment Program: An Interdisciplinary Approach to the Emotionally Disturbed Child." *Child Welfare*, March 1975, pp. 183–194.

Rowe, Mary Potter. "Especially for Working Mothers: How Families Can Help." *Parents Magazine*, April 1978, p. 40.

Rubin, K. H., and Hansen, Rebecca. "Teaching Attitudes and Behaviors of Pre-school Personnel: Curriculum Variations." *Alberta Journal of Educational Research*, September 1976, pp. 261–269.

Saikowski, Charlotte. "The Question Arises—Who Will Raise the Children?" *The Rogers Sunday News*, 29 October 1978.

Schwartz, J. C.; Strickland, R.; and Krolic, G. "Infant Day Care: Behavioral Effects at Preschool Age." *Developmental Psychology* 10 (July 1974): 504.

Serbin, L. A., and O'Leary, K. D. "How Nursery Schools Teach Girls to Shut Up." *Psychology Today*, December 1975, pp. 56–84.

"Sense of Wonder: Parents and Children Learn Together—Science Open House at the Vassar College Laboratory Nursery School." *Southwest Education Digest*, January 1975, pp. 60–62.

Sheehan, Robert, and Day, David. "Is Open Space Just Empty Space?" *Education Digest*, February 1976, pp. 48–50.

Sidel, Ruth. *Women and Child Care in China*. New York: Hill and Wang, 1972.

Smith, Peter, and Green, Maureen. "Aggressive Behavior in English Nurseries and Play Groups: Sex Differences and Response of Adults." *Child Development*, March 1975, pp. 211–214.

Soloman, G. F. "Emotions, Stress, the Central Nervous System and Immunity." *Annals of the New York Academy of Science* 159 (1969): 7.

Spitz, Rene A. "Hospitalism: An Inquiry into the Genesis of Psychiatric Conditions in Early Childhood." *The Psychoanalytic Study of the Child*, Edited by Ruth Eissler, 25 vols. New York: International Universities Press, 1945, 1: 53–74.

Steinfels, M. "Who's Minding the Children?" *Commentary*, 3 December 1974, p. 90.

Strathy, Esther; Heincke, Christoph; and Hauser, Kayla. "The Role of a Social Worker in a Day-Care Center." *Bulletin*, Spring 1974, pp. 25–37.

Sully, Arnold, and Diodati, Anthony. "Ingredients of a Creative Family Day-Care Program." *Child Welfare*, February 1975, pp. 97–101.

Swenson, Janet P. *Alternatives in Quality Care: A Guide for Thinking and Planning*. Washington: Day Care and Child Council of America, 1972.

Van Horne, Harriet. "Working Parents/Wonderful Kids." *Parents Magazine*, April 1978, p. 55.

Waite, L. J., et al. "Changes in Child Care Arrangements of Working Women from 1965 to 1971." *Social Science Quarterly*, September 1977, pp. 302–311.

Winett, Richard A.; Moffatt, Sarah A.; and Fuchs, William L. "Social Issues and Research Strategies in Day Care." *Professional Psychology*, May 1975, pp. 145–154.

Ziai, Mohsen, ed. *Pediatrics*. Boston: Little, Brown and Company, n.d., p. 48.

Abortion

Annas, George J. "Abortion and the Supreme Court: Round Two." *Hastings Center Report*, October 1976.

Arney, W. R., and Trescher, W. H. "Trends in Attitudes Toward Abortion." *Family Planning Perspectives* 8 (May–June 1976): 117.

Barclay, W. R. "Abortion" (editorial). *Journal of American Medical Association*, 16 July 1976, p. 388.

Bajema, Clifford E. *Abortion and the Meaning of Personhood*. Grand Rapids: Baker Book House, 1974.

Bok, Sissela. "The Unwanted Child: Caring of the Fetus Born Alive After An Abortion." *Hastings Center Report*, October 1976, p. 10–15.

Brewer, C. "Incidence of Post-Abortion Psychosis: A Prospective Study." *British Medical Journal*, 19 February 1977, pp. 476–477.

Bryn, R. M. "The New Jurisprudence." *Journal of American Medical Association*, 27 July 1976, pp. 359–360.

Burkle, F. M. "A Development Approach to Post Abortion Depression." *Practitioner*, February 1977, pp. 217–225.

Callahan, S. "The Court and a Conflict of Principles." *Hastings Center Report*, August 1977, pp. 7–8.

Connery, J. R. "Abortion: A Philosophical and Historical Analysis." *Hospital Progress*, April 1977, p. 8.

"The Court and A Conflict of Principles." *Hastings Center Report*, August 1977, pp. 7–8.

Cvejic, H., et al. "Follow-up of 50 Adolescent Girls 2 Years After Abortion." *Canadian Medical Association Journal*, 8 January 1977, pp. 44–46.

Denes, Magda. *In Necessity and Sorrow: Life and Death in an Abortion Hospital*. New York: Penguin Books, 1977.

Evans, J. R., et al. "Teenagers: Fertility Control Behavior and Attitudes Before and After Abortion, Childbearing or Neg-Pregnancy Test." *Family Planning Perspective*, July–August 1976, pp. 192–200.

A Far Cry From Yesterday. Film No. 1022. Available from Planned Parenthood of Southern Arizona, Tucson.

Freeman, E. W. "Influence of Personality Attributes on Abortion Experiences." *American Journal of Orthopsychiatry*, July 1977.

Gerrana, H. "Sex Guilt in Abortion Patients." *Journal of Consulting Clinical Psychology*, August 1977, p. 708.

Greenglass, E. R. "Therapeutic Abortion and Psychiatric Disturbance in Canadian Women." *Canadian Psychiatric Association Journal*, November 1976, pp. 453–460.

Hatcher, S. L. "Understanding Adolescent Pregnancy and Abortion." *Primary Care*, September 1976, pp. 407–425.

Hinthorn, D. R. "When Does Human Life Begin." *Christianity Today*, 24 March 1978, pp. 35–36.

Hurwitz, Arlene, and Eadie, R. Frank. "Psychological Impact on Nursing Students of Participation in Abortion." *Nursing Research*, March–April 1977, pp. 12–20.

Illsley, R., et al. "Psychosocial Aspects of Abortion: A Review of Issued and Needed Research." *Bulletin WHO*, 1976, pp. 83–106.

Leach, J. "The Repeat Abortion Patient." *Family Planning Perspective*, January–February 1977.

Lindheim, B. "Training in Induced Abortion by Obstetrics and Gynecology Residency Programs." *Family Planning Perspective*, January–February 1978.

MacIntyre, S. "To Have or Have Not: Promotion and Prevention of Childbirth in Gynecological Work." *Social Review*, March 1976, pp. 176–193.

Matthews, R. L. "Abortion: A Positive Experience?" *Canadian Medical Association Journal*, 23 April 1977, pp. 836–837.

"Medical Schools and Abortion," *America*, 20 January 1979, p. 23.

McCormick, Richard A. "Abortion: Rules for Debate." *America*, 22 July 1978, p. 29.

Mirande, A. M., et al. "Love, Sex Permissiveness, and Abortion: A Test of Alternate Models." *Archives Sexual Behavior*, November 1976, pp. 553–566.

"Most Abortions by Suction in 10th Week or Less; Typical Patient is Young, Unmarried, White, Never Before Pregnant." *Family Planning Perspective*, March–April 1976, pp. 70–72.

Muller, C. F. "Insurance Coverage of Abortion, Contraception, and Sterilization." *Family Planning Perspectives*, March–April 1978, pp. 71–77.

"The New Jurisprudence." *The Journal of the American Medical Association*, 26 July 1976, p. 359.

Nooman, John T., Jr. "Living Persons, Living Minds." *America*, 3 November 1979, p. 264.

Patt, S. L., et al. "Follow-up of Therapeutic Abortion." *Archives of General Psychiatry*, 1969, pp. 408–414.

Pentecost, A. F. "Effects of Abortion on Obstetric Patterns." *British Medical Journal*, 27 August 1977, p. 578.

Remsberg, Charles and Bonnie. "Second Thoughts on Abortion from the Doctor Who Led the Crusade for It." *Good Housekeeping*, March 1976, p. 69.

Rosoff, J. I. "Pregnancy Counseling and Abortion Referral for Patients in Federally Funded Family Planning Programs." *Family Planning Perspectives* 8 (January–February 1976): 43–46.

Rousseau, Mary F. "Abortion and Intimacy." *America*, 26 May 1979, pp. 429–432.

Segers, M. C. "Abortion and the Supreme Court: Some Are More Equal Than Others." *Hastings Center Report*, August 1977, pp. 5–6.

Simler, S. L. "Three States Are Likely to Continue Abortion Funding for the Medicaid Patient." *Modern Health Care*, August 1977, p. 26.

Simon, N. M., et al. "Psychiatric Illness Following Therapeutic Abortion." *American Journal of Psychiatry*, 1967, pp. 59–65.

Stallworthy, J. A., et al. "Legal Abortion: A Critical Assessment of Its Risks." *The Lancet*, 4 December 1971.

Sullivan, W. F. "Working Together for Christ: Facing the Anti-Life Challenge." *Hospital Progress*, May 1977, pp. 82–84.

Swigar, M. E. "Abortion Applicants: Characteristics Distinguishing Dropouts Remaining Pregnant and Those Having Abortions." *American Journal of Public Health*, July 1977, pp. 621–625.

Tsoi, W. F. et al., "Psychological Effects of Abortion." *Singapore Medical Journal*, June 1976, pp. 68–73.

Uddo, Basil J. "An Inquiry on Abortion." *America*, 14 July 1979, pp. 14–15.

Willke, Jack C., and Willke, Barbara. *Handbook on Abortion*. Cincinnati: Hayes Publishing Co., 1976.

Yankauer, A. "Abortions and Public Policy. Part I and II." *American Journal of Public Health*, July, September 1977.

Marriage & Family

Collins, Gary. *Man In Transition: The Psychology of Human Development*. Carol Stream, Ill.: Creation House, 1971.

Dobson, James. *What Wives Wish Their Husbands Knew About Women*. Wheaton, Ill.: Tyndale House, 1975.

Greenbaum, Henry. "Marriage, Family and Parenthood." *American Journal of Psychiatry*, 131 (November 1973): 1262–1265.

Lidz, Theodore. *The Person*. New York: Basic Books, 1968.

McCandless, Boyd R., and Trotter, Robert J. *Children: Behavior and Development*. 3rd ed. New York: Holt, Rinehart and Winston, 1977.

Meier, Paul D. *Christian Child-Rearing and Personality Development*. Grand Rapids: Baker Book House, 1977.

Minirth, Frank B., and Meier, Paul D. *Happiness Is a Choice*. Grand Rapids: Baker Book House, 1977.

Report of the Fall 1979 Television Monitoring Program of the National Federation for Decency. Box 1398, Tupelo, Miss., 38811.

Voth, Harold. *The Castrated Family*. Mission, Kan.: Sheed Andrews and McMeel, 1977.

"What's Happening to American Morality?" *U.S. News & World Report*, 13 October 1975.

Role of Women

Friedan, Betty. *The Feminine Mystique*. New York: W. W. Norton & Co., 1968.

Galewski, Barbara. "Why I Oppose the ERA—I Saw It in Sweden." *The Women's Lib, Equal Rights Amendment*. Long Beach, Calif.: Concerned Americans, n.d.

Giele, Janet Zollinger. "Changes in the Modern Family: Their Impact on Sex Roles." *American Journal of Orthopsychiatry* 41 (October 1971): 757–766.

Kilgo, Edith Flowers. *Money in the Cookie Jar: The Christian Homemaker's Guide to Making Money at Home*. Grand Rapids: Baker Book House Company, 1980.

Poegrebin, Letty Cottin. "Can Women Really Have It All—Should We?" *Ms*, March 1978, pp. 47–48.

Rowe, Mary Potter. "Especially for Working Mothers: How Families Can Help." *Parents Magazine*, April 1978, p. 40.

Sawikowski, Charlotte. "Moving into Man's World: Tenderness in the Board Room." *The Rogers Sunday News*, 5 November 1978.

Schaeffer, Edith. *Hidden Art*. Wheaton, Ill.: Tyndale House, 1971.

Schlafly, Phyllis. *The Power of the Positive Woman*. New Rochelle: Arlington House, 1977.

Thomson, Rosemary. *The Price of Liberty*. Carol Stream, Ill.: Mansions Press, 1978.